HINTS ON CHILD TRAINING

HINTS ON CHILD TRAINING

H. Clay Trumbull

Wolgemuth & Hyatt, Publishers, Inc.
Brentwood, Tennessee

The mission of Wolgemuth & Hyatt, Publishers, Inc. is to publish and distribute books that lead individuals toward:

- A personal faith in the one true God: Father, Son, and Holy Spirit;
- A lifestyle of practical discipleship; and
- A worldview that is consistent with the historic, Christian faith.

Moreover, the Company endeavors to accomplish this mission at a reasonable profit and in a manner which glorifies God and serves His Kingdom.

Unless otherwise noted, all scripture quotations are from the King James Version of the Bible.

Wolgemuth & Hyatt, Publishers, Inc.
1749 Mallory Lane, Suite 110, Brentwood, Tennessee 37027.

Library of Congress Cataloging-in-Publication Data

Trumbull, H. Clay (Henry Clay), 1830-1903.
    Hints on child training / H. Clay Trumbull.
        p.   cm.
    Reprint, with new introd. Originally published: Philadelphia :
J.D. Wattles, 1891.
    ISBN 0-943497-86-8
    1. Child rearing—Religious aspects—Christianity. 2. Child development. I. Title.
HQ769.3.T78   1990
649'.1—dc20   90-30194
                                                                          CIP

CONTENTS

Foreword / *vii*

Preface / *ix*

1. Child Training: What Is It? / *1*

2. The Duty of Training Children / *5*

3. Scope and Limitations of Child Training / *9*

4. Discerning a Child's Special Need of Training / *13*

5. Will-Training, Rather than Will-Breaking / *19*

6. The Place of "Must" in Training / *29*

7. Denying a Child Wisely / *33*

8. Honoring a Child's Individuality / *39*

9. Letting Alone as a Means of Child Training / *47*

10. Training a Child to Self-Control / *53*

11. Training a Child Not to Tease / *57*

12. Training a Child's Appetite / *63*

13. Training a Child as a Questioner / *69*

14. Training a Child's Faith / *75*

15. Training Children to Sabbath Observance / *81*

16. Training a Child in Amusements / *91*

17. Training a Child to Courtesy / *97*

18. Cultivating a Child's Taste in Reading / *103*

19. The Value of Table Talk / *109*

20. Guiding a Child in Companionships / 115

21. Never Punish a Child in Anger / 121

22. Scolding Is Never in Order / 129

23. Dealing Tenderly with a Child's Fears / 133

24. The Sorrows of Children / 143

25. The Place of Sympathy in Child Training / 149

26. Influence of the Home Atmosphere / 155

27. The Power of a Mother's Love / 159

28. Allowing Play to a Child's Imagination / 167

29. Giving Added Value to a Child's Christmas / 171

30. Good-Night Words / 177

Index / 183

About the Author / 193

FOREWORD

Upon returning to the United States after serving a mission term in England, my wife Karen and I founded the Charlotte Mason Research and Supply Company.

Our first major project involved finding and republishing the complete works of British educator and child expert Charlotte Mason. The response from parents was so great for this type of classic writing, it occurred to us there must be other valuable and rare child raising books from long ago that speak to parents as clearly today as when first published. So after many months of research and careful evaluation, we have unearthed yet another practical treasure in this one-volume guide, *Hints on Child Training* by Henry Clay Trumbull, originally written in 1890. H. C. Trumbull was one of America's most prominent Christian authors and spokesmen, dedicated to the evangelism of children. It was his love for children and a goal to see peace and order brought back to our homes that prompted the writing of this book. He shares very frankly from his lifetime experience with teaching children and raising eight children of his own. These are working principles and not untried theories.

What we appreciate most about *Hints on Child Training* is how clear, easy to read, and very practical it is.

Trumbull does not confuse issues, water down his main points, or tell long unnecessary stories for his illustrations. You do not have to read through many chapters to glean a few good ideas (like many books today). Each chapter can stand on its own and is filled with great practical advice. You can readily remember what you've read and then try it with your children, with remarkably quick results. Parents will find this book very refreshing. He emphasizes, in plain language, the greatest concerns of parents as well as teachers, homeschoolers, and child experts today—character development, discipline, courtesy, parental love, cultivating good reading habits, quality family and holiday time, Bible Illustrations, etc.

This book lays the foundations for child training that will last a lifetime. It will improve your attitude toward your child. Your child will develop greater respect and trust in you. These simple principles put into practice will draw families closer together and allow God's blessing to be more clearly manifest in our homes.

It is our hope that many will find happiness restored to their hurting families as they read *Hints on Child Training*. We believe you will be blessed by this book and will want to share it with others.

So, welcome back, H. C. Trumbull, after too long an absence.

Sincerely,
Dean and Karen Andreola

If you would like to share your comments on *Hints and Child Training*, or keep posted on current and future projects of this nature, send a self-addressed stamped envelope to:

Charlotte Mason Research and Supply Company
P.O. Box 172
Stanton, NJ 08885

PREFACE

Hints on child training may be helpful, where a formal treatise on the subject would prove bewildering. It is easier to see how one phase or another of children's needs is to be met, than it is to define the relation of that phase of the case to all other phases, or to a system that includes them all. Therefore it is that this series of Hints is ventured by me for the benefit of young parents, although I would not dare attempt a systematic treatise on the entire subject here touched upon.

Thirty years ago, when I was yet a young father, a friend, who knew that I had for years been interested in the study of methods of education, said to me, "Trumbull, what is your theory of child training?" "Theory?" I responded. "I have no theory in that matter. I had lots of theories before I had any children; but now I do, with fear and trembling, in every case just that which seems to be the better thing for the hour, whether it agrees with any of my old theories or not."

Whatever theory of child training may show itself in these Hints, has been arrived at by induction in the process of my experiences with children since I had to deal with the matter practically, apart from any preconceived view of the principles involved. Every suggestion in these Hints is an outcome of experiment and observation in my life as a father and a grandfather, while it has been carefully considered in the light of the best lessons of practical educators on every side.

These Hints were begun for the purpose of giving help to a friend. They were continued because of the evident popular interest in them. They are sent out in this completed form in the hope that they will prove of service to parents who are feeling the need of something more practical in the realm of child training than untested theories.

H. Clay Trumbull

PHILADELPHIA, *September* 15, 1890

ONE

CHILD TRAINING: WHAT IS IT?

The term "training," like the term "teaching," is used in various senses; hence it is liable to be differently understood by different persons, when applied to a single department of a parent's duties in the bringing up of his children. Indeed, the terms "training" and "teaching" are often used interchangeably, as covering the entire process of a child's education. In this sense a child's training is understood to include his teaching; and, again, his teaching is understood to include his training. But in its more restricted sense the training of a child is the shaping, the developing, and the controlling of his personal faculties and powers; while the teaching of a child is the securing to him of knowledge from beyond himself.

It has been said that the essence of teaching is causing another to *know*. It may similarly be said that the essence of training is causing another to *do*. Teaching gives knowledge. Training gives skill. Teaching fills the mind. Training shapes the habits. Teaching brings to the child that which he did not have before. Training enables a child to make use of that which is already his possession. We teach a child the meaning of words. We train a child in speaking and walking.

We teach him the truths which we have learned for ourselves. We train him in habits of study, that he may be able
to learn other truths for himself. Training and teaching
must go on together in the wise upbringing of any and every
child. The one will fail of its own best end if it be not accom-
panied by the other. He who knows how to teach a child, is
not competent for the oversight of a child's education unless
he also knows how to train a child.

Training is a possibility long before teaching is. Before
a child is old enough to know what is said to it, it is capable of feeling, and of conforming to, or of resisting, the pressure of efforts for its training. A child can be trained to go
to sleep in the arms of its mother or nurse, or in a cradle,
or on a bed; with rocking, or without it; in a light room, or
in a dark one; in a noisy room, or only in a quiet one; to
expect nourishment and to accept it only at fixed hours,
or at its own fancy, — while as yet it cannot understand any
teaching concerning the importance or the fitness of one
of these things. A very young child can be trained to cry
for what it wants, or to keep quiet, as a means of securing
it. And, as a matter of fact, the training of children is begun much earlier than their teaching. Many a child is well
started in its life-training by the time it is six weeks old; even
though its elementary teaching is not attempted until months
after that.

There is a lesson just at this point in the signification of
the Hebrew word translated "train" in our English Bible. It
is a noteworthy fact, that this word occurs only twice in the
Old Testament, and it has no equivalent in the New. Those
who were brought up in the household of Abraham, "the
father of the faithful," are said to have been "trained" (Gen.
14:14). A proverb of the ages gives emphasis to a parent's
duty to "train up" his child with wise consideration (Prov.
22:6). And nowhere else in the inspired record does the
original of this word "train," in any of its forms, appear.

The Hebrew word thus translated is a peculiar one. Its etymology shows that its primary meaning is "to rub the gullet"; and its origin seems to have been in the habit, still prevalent among primitive peoples, of opening the throat of a new-born babe by the anointing of it with blood, or with saliva, or with some sacred liquid, as a means of giving the child a start in life by the help of another's life. The idea of the Hebrew word thus used seems to be that, as this opening of the gullet of a child at its very birth is essential to the habituating of the child to breathe and to swallow correctly, so the right training of a child in all proper habits of life is to begin at the child's very birth. And the use of the word in the places where we find it, would go to show that Abraham with all his faith, and Solomon with all his wisdom, did not feel that it would be safe to put off the start of a child's training any later than this.

Child training properly begins at a child's birth, but it does not properly end there. The first effort in the direction of child training is to train a child to breathe and to swallow; but that ought not to be the last effort in the same direction. Child training goes on as long as a child is a child; and child training covers every phase of a child's action and bearing in life. Child training affects a child's sleeping and waking, his laughing and crying, his eating and drinking, his looks and his movements, his self-control and his conduct toward others. Child training does not change a child's nature, but it does change his modes of giving expression to his nature. Child training does not give a child entirely new characteristics, but it brings him to the repression and subduing of certain characteristics, and to the expression and development of certain others, to such an extent that the sum of his characteristics presents an aspect so different from its original exhibit that it seems like another character. And so it is that child training is, in a sense, like the very making of a child anew.

Child training includes the directing and controlling and shaping of a child's feelings and thoughts and words and ways in every sphere of his life-course, from his birth to the close of his childhood. And that this is no unimportant part of a child's upbringing, no intelligent mind will venture to question.

THE DUTY OF TRAINING CHILDREN

I t is the mistake of many parents to suppose that their chief duty is in loving and counseling their children, rather than in loving and training them; that they are faithfully to show their children what they ought to do, rather than to make them do it. The training power of the parent is, as a rule, sadly undervalued.

Too many parents seem to take it for granted that because their children are by nature very timid and retiring, or very bold or forward; very extravagant in speech and manner, or quite disinclined to express even a dutiful sense of gratitude and trust; reckless in their generosity, or pitiably selfish; disposed to overstudy, or given wholly to play; one-sided in this, or in that, or in the other, trait or quality or characteristic—therefore those children must remain so; unless, indeed, they outgrow their faults, or are induced by wise counsel and loving entreaty to overcome them.

"My boy is irrepressible," says one father. "He is full of dash and spirits. He makes havoc in the house while at home; and when he goes out to a neighbor's he either has things his own way, or he doesn't want to go *there* again. I really wish he had a quieter nature; but, of course, I can't change him. I have given him a great many talks about this; and I hope he will outgrow the worst of it. Still he is just what he is, and punishing him wouldn't make him anybody else." A good mother, on the other hand, is exercised because her little son is so bashful that he is always mortifying her before strangers. He will put his finger in his mouth, and hang down his head, and twist one foot over the other, and refuse to shake hands, or to answer the visitor's "How do you do, my boy?" or even to say, "I thank you," with distinctness, when anything is given to him. And the same trouble is found with the tastes as with the temperaments of children. One is always ready to hear stories read or told, but will not sit quiet and look at pictures, or use a slate and pencil. Another, a little older, will devour books of travel or adventure, but has no patience with a simple story of home life, or a book of instruction in matters of practical fact.

Now it is quite inevitable that children should have these peculiarities; but it is not inevitable that they should continue to exhibit them offensively. Children can be trained in almost any direction. Their natural tendencies may be so curbed and guided as no longer to show themselves in disagreeable prominence. It is a parent's privilege, and it is a parent's duty, to make his children, by God's blessing, to be and to do what they should be and do, rather than what they would like to be and do. If indeed this were not so, a parent's mission would be sadly limited in scope, and diminished in importance and preciousness. The parent who does not recognize the possibility of training his children as well as instructing them, misses one of his highest privileges as a parent, and fails in his most important work for his children.

The skilled physician in charge of a certain institution for the treatment of developmentally disabled and imperfectly developed children, has said, that some children who are brought to him are lacking in just one important trait or quality, while they possess a fair measure of every other. Or it may be said, that they have an excess of the trait or quality opposite to that which they lack.

One girl, for example, will be wholly without a sense of honesty; will even be possessed with a love of stealing for stealing's sake, carrying it to such an extent that when seated at the table she will snatch a ball of butter from a plate, and wrap it up in a fold of her dress. If she should be unchecked in this propensity until she were a grown woman, she might prove one of the fashionable ladies who take books or dry goods from the stores where they are shopping, under the influence of "kleptomania."

Again, a boy has no sense of truth. He will tell lies without any apparent temptation to do so, even against his own obvious interests. All of us have seen persons of this sort in mature life. Some of them are today in places of prominence in Christian work and influence. Yet another child is without any sense of reverence, or of modesty, or of natural affection. One lacks all control of his temper, another of his nerves. And so on in great variety.

The physician of that institution is by no means in despair over any of these cases. It is his mission to find out the child's special lack, and to meet it; to learn what traits are in excess, and to curb them; to know the child's needs, and to *train* him accordingly.

Every child is in a sense a partially developed, an imperfectly formed child. There are no absolutely perfect children in this world. All of them need restraining in some things and stimulating in others. And every imperfect child can be helped toward a symmetrical character by wise Christian training. Every home should be an institution for the treatment of imperfectly developed children. Every father and every mother should be a skilled physician in charge of such an institution. There are glorious possibilities in this direction; and there are weighty responsibilities also.

THREE

SCOPE AND LIMITATIONS OF CHILD TRAINING

Child training can compass much, but child training cannot compass everything, in determining the powers and the possibilities of a child under training. Each child can be trained in the way *he* should go, but not every child can be trained to go in the same way. Each child can be trained to the highest and fullest exercise of *his* powers, but no child can be trained to the exercise of powers which are not his. Each child can be trained to *his* utmost possibilities, but not every child can be trained to the utmost possibilities of every other child. Child training has the fullest scope of the capacity of the particular child under treatment, and child training is limited in every case by the limitations of that child's capacity.

A child born blind can be trained to such a use of his other senses that he can do more in the world than many a poorly trained child who has sight; but a blind child can never be trained to discern differences in colors at a distance. A child who has by nature a dull ear for music can be trained to more or less of musical skill; but a child who is born without the sense of hearing can never be trained to quickness in the discerning of sounds. A child can be trained to facility in the use of every sense and faculty and limb and member and muscle and nerve which he possesses; but no training will give to a child a new sense, a new faculty, a new limb, a new member, a new muscle, a new nerve. Child training can make anything of a child that can be made of that child, but child training cannot change a child's nature and identity.

The limitations of child training are more likely to be realized than its extensive scope. Indeed, the supposed limitations of child training are very often unreal ones. Many a parent would say, for example, that you cannot change a child's form and features and expression by training; yet, as a matter of fact, a child's form and features and expression can be, and often are, materially changed by training. The chest is expanded, the waist is compressed, a curved spine is straightened, or a deformity of limb is corrected, by persistent training with the help of mechanical appliances. Among some primitive peoples, the form of every child's head is brought to a conventional standard by a process of training; as, among other primitive peoples, the feet or the ears or the eyes or the lips are thus conventionally trained into—or out of—shape. And in all lands the expression of the face steadily changes under the process of persistent training.

As it is with the physical form, so it is with the mental and moral characteristics of a child; the range is wide within the limitations of possible results from the training process. A nervous temperament cannot, it is true, be trained into a phlegmatic one, or a phlegmatic temperament be trained into a nervous one; but a child who is quick and impulsive can be trained into moderation and carefulness of speech and of action, while a child who is sluggish and inactive can be trained to rapidity of movement and to energy of endeavor. An imbecile mind can never be trained into the possibilities of native genius, nor can a moral nature of the lowest order be trained to the same measure of high conscientiousness as a nature that is keenly sensitive to every call of duty and to the rights and feelings of others; but training can give unsuspected power to the dormant faculties of the dullminded, and can marvelously develop the latent moral sense of any child who is capable of discerning between right and wrong in conduct.

The sure limitations of a child's possibilities of training are obvious to a parent. If one of the physical senses be lacking to the child, no training will restore that sense, although wise training may enable the child to overcome many of the difficulties that meet him as a consequence of his native lack. And so, also, if the child have such unmistakable defects of mind and of character as prove him to be inferior to the ordinary grade of average humanity, the wisest training cannot be expected to lift him above the ordinary level of average humanity. But if a child be in the possession of the normal physical senses, and the normal mental faculties, and the normal moral capacities, of the human race, he may, by God's blessing, be trained to the best and fullest use of his powers in these several spheres, in spite of all the hindrances and drawbacks that are found in the perversion or the imperfect development of those powers at his start in life.

In other words, if the child be grievously deformed or defective at birth, or by some early casualty, there is an inevitable limitation accordingly to the possibilities of his training. But if a child be in possession of an ordinary measure of faculties and capacity, his training will decide the manner and method and extent of the use of his God-given powers.

It is, therefore, largely a child's training that settles the question whether a child is graceful or awkward in his personal movements, gentle or rough in his ways with his fellows, considerate or thoughtless in his bearing toward others; whether he is captious or tractable within the bounds of due restraint; whether he is methodical and precise, or unsystematic and irregular, in the discharge of his daily duties; whether he is faithful in his studies, or is neglectful of them; whether he is industrious or indolent in his habits; whether the tastes which he indulges in his diet and dress and reading and amusements and companionships are refined, or are low. In all these things his course indicates what his training has been; or it suggests the training that he needed, but has missed.

FOUR

DISCERNING A CHILD'S SPECIAL NEED OF TRAINING

Some one has said, that a mother is quite right when she declares enthusiastically of her little one, "There never was such a child as this, in the world, before!" for in fact there never before was such a child. Each child starts in life as if he were the only child in the world, and the first one; and he is less like other people then than ever he will be again. He is conformed to no regulation pattern at the outset. He has, to begin with, no stock of ideas which have been passed on and approved by others. He neither knows nor cares what other people think. He is a law unto himself in all matters of thought and taste and feeling. He is, so far, himself; and, just so far, he is different from everybody else.

Left to himself, if that were a possibility, every child would continue to be himself; but no child is left to himself: he is under training and in training continually. And so it is that the training of a child is quite as likely to change him from his best self to a poorer self, as it is to develop and perfect that which is best in his distinctive self. Child training is, in many a case, the bringing of a child into purely conventional ways, instead of bringing out into freest play, in the child, those qualities and characteristics which mark him as a unique and individual personality among the sons of men. How to learn wherein it needs curbing or changing, is a question of questions in child training.

No quality of a good physician is of more importance than skill in making a diagnosis of a patient's case. If a mastermind in this realm were to pass with positiveness on the disease of every patient, the treatment of that disease would be comparatively easy. A young graduate from the medical school, or a trained nurse, would then, in most instances, be capable of knowing and doing that which was needful in the premises. But until the diagnosis is accurate, the best efforts of the ablest physician are liable to be misdirected, and so to be ineffective for good. As it is with the physician and his patient, so it is with the parent and his child. An accurate diagnosis is an essential prerequisite to wise and efficient treatment. The diagnosis secured, the matter of treatment is a comparatively easy matter. A parent's diagnosis of his child's case is in the discerning of his child's faults, as preliminary to a process of training for their cure. Until *that* is secured, there is no hope of intelligent and well-directed treatment.

Yet it is not the easiest thing in the world to say what are a child's peculiar faults, and what is, therefore, that child's peculiar need of training. Many a parent is disturbed by a child's best traits, while he underestimates or overlooks that child's chief failings. And many another parent who knows that his child is full of faults cannot say just what they are, or classify them according to their relative prominence and their power for evil. "That boy's questions will worry my life out. He is always asking questions; and *such* questions. I can't stand it!" This is said by many a father or mother whose child is full of promise, largely because he is full of questions.

But if a boy has a bright mind and positive preferences, and is ready to study or to work untiringly in the line of his own tastes, and in no other line, it does not always occur to his parents that just here—in this reluctance to apply himself in the line of wise expediency rather than of personal fancy—there is a failing which, if not trained out of that boy, will stand as a barrier to his truest manhood, and will make him a second-rate man when he might be a first-rate one; a one-sided man instead of a well-proportioned man. Such a boy is quite likely to be looked upon as one who must be permitted to have his own way, since that way is evidently not a bad way, and he shows unusual power in its direction. So that boy may be left untrained in this particular until he is hopelessly past training, merely because his chief fault is unrecognized by those who could correct it, and who would gladly do so if they saw it in its due proportions.

Careful study and a wise discrimination are needed on a parent's part to ascertain a child's peculiar faults. Each parent would do well to ask himself, or herself, the questions, "What are the special faults of my child? Where is he weakest? In what direction is his greatest strength liable to lead him astray, and when is it most likely to fail him? Which of his faults is most prominent? Which of them is of chief importance for immediate correction?" Such questions as these should be considered at a time favorable to deliberate judgment, when there is least temptation to be influenced by personal feeling, either of preference or dissatisfaction. They should be pondered long and well.

The unfriendly criticisms of neighbors, and the kind suggestions of friends, are not to be despised by a parent in making up an estimate of his child's failings and faults. Rarely is a parent so discerning, so impartial, and so wise, that he can know his children through and through, and be able to weigh the several traits, and perceive the every imperfection and exaggeration, of their characters, with unerring accuracy and absolute fairness. A judge is supposed to be disqualified for an impartial hearing of a case in which he has a direct personal interest. A physician will not commonly make a diagnosis of his own disorders, lest his fears or hopes should bias his judgment. And a parent is as liable as a judge or a physician to be swayed unduly by interest or affection, in an estimate of a case which is before him for a decision.

Even though, therefore, every parent must decide for himself concerning the interests and the treatment of his own children, he ought to be glad to take into consideration what others think and say of those children, while he is making up his mind as to his duty in the premises. And what is written or said on this subject by competent educators is worthy of attention from every parent who would train his children understandingly. There is little danger that any parent will give too much study to the question of his child's specific needs, or have too many helps to a wise conclusion on that point. There is a great deal of danger that the whole subject will be neglected or undervalued by a parent.

If a parent were explicitly to ask the question of a fair and plain-speaking friend, familiar with that parent's children, and competent to judge them, "What do you think is the chief fault—or the most objectionable characteristic—of my son—or daughter?" the frank answer to that question would in very many cases be an utter surprise to the parent, the fault or characteristic named not having been suspected by the parent. A child may be so much like the parent just here, that the parent's blindness to his or her own chief fault or lack may forbid the seeing of the child's similar deformity. Or, again, that child may be so totally unlike the parent, that the parent will be unable to appreciate, or even to apprehend, that peculiarity of the child which is apparent to every outside intelligent observer. A child's reticence from deep feeling has often been counted by an over-demonstrative parent as a sign of want of sensitiveness; and so *vice versa.*

Parents need help from others, from personal friends whom they can trust to speak with impartiality and kindness, or from the teachers of their children, in the gaining of a proper estimate and understanding of their children's characteristics and needs. The parent who does not realize this truth, and act on it, will never do as well as might be done for his or her child. God has given the responsibility of the training of that child to the parent; but He has also laid on that parent the duty of learning, by the aid of all proper means, what are the child's requirements, and how to meet them.

FIVE

WILL-TRAINING, RATHER THAN WILL-BREAKING

The measure of willpower is the measure of personal power, with a child as with an adult. The possession or the lack of willpower is the possession or the lack of personal power, in every individual's sphere of life and being. The right or the wrong use of willpower is the right or the wrong exercise of an individual's truest personality. Hence the careful guarding and the wise guiding of a child's will should be counted among the foremost duties of one who is responsible for a child's training.

Will-training is an important element in child training; but will-breaking has no part or place in the training of a child. A broken will is worth as much in its sphere as a broken bow; just that, and no more. A child with a broken will is not so well furnished for the struggle of life as a child with only one arm, or one leg, or one eye. Such a child has no power of strong personality, or of high achievement in the world. Every child ought to be trained to conform his will to the demands of duty; but that is bending his will, not breaking it. Breaking a child's will is never in order.

The term "will" as here employed applies to a child's faculty of choosing or deciding between two courses of action.

Breaking a child's will is bringing the pressure of external force directly upon that will, causing the will to give way under the pressure of that force. Training a child's will is bringing such influences to bear upon the child that he is ready to choose or decide in favor of the right course of action.

To break a child's will is to crush out for the time being, and so far to destroy, the child's privilege of free choice; it is to force him to an action against his choice, instead of inducing him to choose in the right direction. A child's will is his truest personality; the expression of his will in a free choice is the highest expression of his personality. And a child's personality is to be held sacred by God's representative who is over the child, even as God Himself holds sacred the personality of every human being created in the image of God.

God never says unqualifiedly to a human being, "You shall not exercise your faculty of choice between the way of life and the way of death; you shall walk in the way which I know to be best for you." But, on the contrary, God says to every one (Deut. 30:15): "See, I have set before thee this day life and good, and death and evil,"—for thy choice. Here, as everywhere, God concedes to man the privilege of exercising his willpower in the direction of life and good, or of death and evil. The strictest Calvinist and the broadest Arminian are at one in their opinion so far. Whatever emphasis is laid, in their philosophy, on God's influencing or enabling the human will to its final choice, neither of them disputes the fact that man is actually permitted to use that will in the direction of his choice. "It is God that worketh *in* man to *will* and to work for His good pleasure." It is not that God worketh above man to crush out man's faculty of willing whether to act for or against His good pleasure. In other words, God has foreordained that every man shall have the freedom of his will—and take the consequences.

It is true that God holds out before man, as an inducement to him in his choosing, the inevitable results of his

choice. If he chooses good, life comes with it. If he chooses
evil, death is its accompaniment. The rewards and the punishments are declared in advance; but after all, and in spite
of all, the choice is man's own. And every soul shall have
eternally the destiny of its own choosing. The representative
of God clothed with power, as he stood before the people of
Israel, did not say, "You *shall* choose God's service now; and
if you deliberately refuse to do so, God will break your will
so that you do do it"; but He said, "If it seem evil unto you to
serve the LORD, choose you this day whom ye will serve"
(Josh. 24:15).

As God, our wise and loving Father in heaven, deals with
us His children, so we, as earthly fathers, should deal with
our children. We should guard sacredly their privilege of
personal choice; and while using every proper means to in-
duce them to choose aright, we should never, never, never
force their choice, even into the direction of our intelligent
preference for them. The final responsibility of a choice and of
its consequences rests with the child, and not with the parent.

A child's will ought to be strong for right-doing. If it be
not so at the start, it is the parent's duty to guide, or train, it
accordingly. But to break, or crush, a child's will, is inconsistent with the educating and training of that will. A conflict between a parent and a child, where the only question
is, "Whose will shall yield to the other?" is, after all, neither
more nor less than a conflict of brute force.

Whether, in any instance, the will of the parent be set on
having his child commit some repulsive crime against which
the child's moral nature recoils, or whether the will of the
parent be set on the child's reciting a Bible text or saying a
prayer, the mere conflict of wills as a conflict of wills is a conflict of brute force; and in such a conflict neither party
ought to succeed,—for success in any such case is always a
failure. If the parent really wills that the child shall do right,
the parent's endeavor should be to have the child will in the

same direction. Merely to force one will into subjection to the other is, however, an injury both to the one who forces and to the one who submits.

A hypothetical illustration may make this matter clearer. A father says to his strong-willed child: "Johnny, shut that door." Johnny says, "I won't." The father says, "You shall." Johnny rejoins, "I won't." An issue is here made between two wills—the father's and the son's. Many a parent would suppose that in such a case the child's will ought to be broken, subjugated, forced, if need be, under the pressure of the father's will; and the more conscientious the parent, the firmer is likely to be his conviction of duty accordingly.

It is at such a point as this that the evil of breaking a child's will, instead of training it, finds its foothold in many a Christian home. The father is determined not to yield his will to his child's will. The child is determined not to yield his will to his father's will. It is the old conflict between "an irresistible force and an immovable body." In such a case, brute force may compel the child to do that which he chooses not to do, just as the rack and thumbscrews of the Inquisition could compel the tortured one to deny a belief which he chooses to adhere to; but in the one case, as in the other, the victim of the torturing pressure is permanently harmed, while the cause of truth and right has been in no sense the gainer by the triumph. Oh, what if God should treat His children in that way!

What, then, it may be asked, should be done with such a child in an issue like this? It certainly would have been better, it would have been far better, for the parent not to make a direct issue by following the child's first refusal with the unqualified declaration, "You shall." But with the issue once made, however unfortunately, then what? Let the parent turn to the child in loving gentleness,—not *then* in severity, and never, never, never in *anger*,—and tell him tenderly of a better way than that which he is pursuing, urging him to a wiser, nobler choice. In most cases the very absence of any show of angry conflict on the father's part will prompt the child to choose to do that which he said he would not do. But if worst comes to worst (for we are here taking the most extreme supposed issue, which ought indeed rarely, if ever, to occur), let the parent say to the child: "Johnny, I shall have to give you your choice in this matter. You can either shut that door or take a whipping." Then a new choice is before the boy, and his will is free and unbroken for its meeting.

Be it understood, the father has no right to say, "I will whip you until you shut that door"; for that would be to deprive the boy of a choice, to deprive the boy of his willpower in the direction of his action: and that no parent is ever justified in doing. If the boy chooses to be whipped rather than to obey, the father must accept the result so far, and begin again for the next time; although, of course, there must be no undue severity in a child's punishment; even the civil law forbids that. The father as a father is not entitled to have his will stand in the place of his child's will; even though he is privileged to strive to bring the child to will in the same direction that the father's will trends.

All the way along through his training-life, a child ought to know what are to be the legitimate consequences of his chosen action, in every case, and then be privileged to choose accordingly. There is a place for punishment in a child's training, but punishment is a penalty attached to a choice; it is not brute force applied to compel action against choice. No child ought ever to be punished, unless he understood, when he chose to do the wrong in question, that he was thereby incurring the penalty of that punishment.

In most cases it is better, as has been said, for a parent to *avoid* a direct issue with a child, than to seek, or even than to recognize and meet, an issue. And in the endeavor to train a child's will, there is often a gain in giving the child an alternative consequence of obedience or disobedience. *That* is God's way of holding out rewards and punishments. For example, a wise young mother was just giving her little boy a bit of candy which was peculiarly prized by him, when, in speaking to a lady visitor he called her by the familiar term used by older members of the family in addressing her. The mother reminded him of the manner in which he should speak to the lady. He refused to conform to this. "Then I cannot let you have this candy," said the mother. "All right," was the willful reply. "I'd rather go without the candy than call her what you tell me to." The mother turned quietly away, taking the candy with her. An hour later that child came to his mother, saying, "Mamma, perhaps you can give me that candy now; for I will always call that lady just what you tell me to." A few added words from the mother at that juncture settled that point for all time. Thenceforward the child did as he had thus been led to will to do. His will had not been broken, but it had been newly directed by judicious training.

But, it may be asked, if a child be told by his mother to leave the room, at a time when it is peculiarly important that he should not remain there, and he says that he will not go, what shall be done with him? Shall he be permitted to have his own way, against his own true welfare? If the chief point be to get him out of the room, and there is no time just then for his training, the child can be carried out by main strength. But that neither breaks nor trains the child's will. It is not a triumph of will, but of muscle. The child, in such a case, leaves the room against his will, and in spite of it. His will has simply been ignored, not broken. And there are times when a child's bodily removal from one place to another is more important for the time being than is, just then, the child's will-training. Such would be the case if the house were on fire, or if the child were taken suddenly ill. But that is apart from the question of will-training or will-breaking. The distinction here noted ought not to be lost sight of in considering this question.

If, however, in the case above cited, the purpose of the mother be to meet the issue which is there raised, and to have it settled once for all whose will shall triumph, right or wrong, the mother can bring the pressure of brute force to bear on the child's will, in order to its final breaking. Under that pressure, the child's life may go out before his will is broken. In many an instance of that sort, this has been the result. Or, again, the child's will may then be broken. If it be so, the child is harmed for life; and so is his mother. The one has come into a slavish submission to the conscientiously tyrannical demands of the other. Both have obtained wrong conceptions of parental authority, wrong conceptions of filial obedience, and wrong conceptions of the plan and methods of the Divine-Parental government. But if, on the other hand, now be the time for teaching a child to use his own will aright, at the summons of one who is older and wiser than himself, and who is over him in the plan of God for his guidance and training, there is a better way than either the forcing a child out of the room against his will, or the breaking of his will so that that will is powerless to prompt him to stay or to go.

The course to be pursued in this case is that already suggested in the case of the child whose father told him to shut the door. Let the mother give herself, at once, to firm and gentle endeavors to bring that child to use his own will, freely and gladly, in the direction of her commands to him. If necessary, let there be no more of sleeping or eating in that home until that child, under the forceful pressure of wise counsel and of affectionate entreaty, has willed to do that which he ought to do, — has willed to be an obedient child. Here, again, is the difference between the wise training of the will, and the always unwise and unjustifiable breaking of the will.

Even in the matter of dealing with the lower animals, it has been found that the old idea of "breaking" the will as a substitute for, or as a necessary precedent of, the "training" the will, is an erroneous one; and the remarkable power of such horse-trainers as Rarey and Gleason grows out of the fact that they are *trainers*, and not *breakers*, of horses. A standard work on dog training, by S. T. Hammond, is based on the idea, indicated in one of its titles, of "Training *versus* Breaking." It might seem, indeed, that the counsel of this latter writer, concerning the wise treatment of a young dog taken newly in hand for his training, were given to a parent concerning the wise treatment of a young child when first taken in hand for this purpose.

"Do not fail to abundantly caress him and speak kindly words," he says; "and never under any circumstances, no matter what the provocation, allow yourself to scold, or [in this early stage] strike him, as this is entirely at variance with our system, and is sure to result in the defeat of our plans. . . . Be very gentle with him at all times. Carefully study his disposition, and learn all of his ways, that you may the more readily understand just how to manage him. You should be in perfect sympathy with him, and humor all his whims and notions, and endeavor to teach him that you truly love him. In a short time you will find that this love will be returned tenfold, and that he is ever anxiously watching for your coming, and never so happy as when in your presence and enjoying your caresses." This, be it borne in mind, is in a line of work that seeks to bring the entire will of the trained in loving subjection to the will of the trainer. And that which is none too high a standard for a young dog ought not to be deemed too high for attainment by a rational child.

Surely that which is found to be the best way for a trainer of dogs on the one hand, and which, on the other hand, is God's way with all His children, may fairly be recognized as both practicable and best for a human parent's dealing with his intelligent little ones. And all this is written by one who in well-nigh forty years of parental life has tried more than one way in child training, and who long ago learned by experience as well as by study that God's way in this thing is unmistakably the best way.

SIX

THE PLACE OF "MUST" IN TRAINING

With all the modern improvements in methods of dealing with children—and these improvements are many and great—it is important to bear in mind that judicious *discipline* has an important part in the wise training of the young. Discipline is not everything in the sphere of child training; but discipline is much, in that sphere. Discipline is an important factor in will-training; and will-training is an important factor in wise child training, although will-breaking is not.

Formerly, discipline was the greater feature, if not, indeed, the only feature, in the training of children. There was a time when children were not allowed to sit in the presence of their parents, or to speak to them unless they were first spoken to, or to have a place with their parents at the home table or in the church pew; when the approved mode of teaching was a primitive and very simple one. "They told a child to learn; and if he did not, they beat him." The school-days of children were then spoken of as "when they were under the rod." Even the occasional celebration of a holy day did not bring unalloyed delight to the little ones; as, for instance, "on Innocents' Day, an old custom of our ancestors was to flog the poor children in their beds, not as a punishment, but to impress on their minds the murder of the innocents."

But all this is in the long past. For a century or more the progress of interest in and attention to the children has been steady and rapid. And now the best talent of the world is laid under contribution for the little ones. In the provisions of song and story and pictures and toys and games, as well as in school buildings and school appliances and school methods, the place of the children is foremost. At home they certainly do not hesitate to sit down when and where they please, or to speak without waiting to be spoken to. Indeed, there are parents who wonder if *they* will ever get a chance to sit down while their children are in the house; or if ever those children will stop asking questions. Meanwhile in secular schools and in Sunday schools the aim seems to be to make learning as attractive as possible to children, and to relieve study, as far as may be, of all tediousness and discomfort.

Now, that this state of things is, on the whole, a decided improvement over that which it displaced, there is no room for fair doubt. Yet there is always a danger of losing sight of one important truth in the effort to give new and due prominence to another. Hence attention should be given to the value of judicious discipline in the training of children. Children need to learn how to do things which they do not want to do, when those things ought to be done. Older people have to do a great many things from a sense of duty. Unless children are trained to recognize duty as more binding than inclination, they will suffer all their lives through from their lack of discipline in this direction.

Children ought to be trained to get up in the morning at a proper hour, for some other reason than that this is to be "the maddest, merriest day in all the glad new year." They ought to learn to go to bed at a fitting time, whether they are sleepy or not. Their hours of eating, and the quality and quantity of their food, ought to be regulated by some other standard than their inclinations. In their daily life there must be a place for tasks as tasks, for times of study under the pressure of stern duty, in the effort to train them to do their right work properly. It is not enough to have children learn only lessons which they enjoy, and this at times and by methods which are peculiarly pleasing to them. President Porter, of Yale, said, in substance, that the chief advantage of the college curriculum is, that it trains a young man to do what he ought to do, when he ought to do it, whether he wants to do it or not. Any course of training for a young person that fails to accomplish thus much, is part of a sadly imperfect system.

There are few, if any, children who do not need to be trained to apply themselves earnestly to occupations which they dislike. The tastes of some children are very good, and of others very poor; but nearly all children have positive inclinations in one direction or in another. They like playing better than working or reading; or they prefer reading or working to playing. Some prefer to remain indoors; others prefer to be outside. Some want to occupy themselves always in mechanical pursuits; others would always be at games of one sort or another. Some enjoy being with companions; others prefer to be by themselves; yet others would attach themselves to one or two persons only, having little care for the society of anybody else. In their studies, children show, perhaps very early, a decided fancy for geography, or history, or mathematics, or the languages, and a pronounced distaste for other branches of learning. Now, whether a child's tastes are elevated or unrefined, in the direction of better or more undesirable pursuits, he ought not to be permitted to follow always his own fancies, or to do only that which he really likes to do.

The parent or the teacher must decide what pursuit of activity, or what branch of study, is best for each child, and must train him to it accordingly. In making this decision, it is important to consider fully the tastes and peculiarities of the particular child under training; but the decision itself must rest with the guardian rather than with the child. Whatever place "elective" studies may properly have in a university curriculum, there is need of positive limitations to the elective system of duties in the nursery and in the home sphere generally.

Hardly anything can be more important in the mental training of a child than the bringing him to do what he ought to do, and to do it in its proper time, whether he enjoys doing it or not. The measure of a child's ability to do this becomes, in the long run, the measure of his practical efficiency in whatever sphere of life he labors. No man can work always merely in the line of his personal preferences. He must do many things which are distasteful to him. Unless he was trained as a child to do such things persistently, he cannot do them to advantage when they are upon him as a necessity. Nor can any man do his best work as well as he ought to, if he works always and only in one line. A one-sided man is not a well-balanced man, even though his one side be the right side. It is better to use the dextral hand than the sinister, but it is certainly preferable to be ambidextrous.

There is little danger that intelligent Christian parents or teachers will at this day refuse to consider duly a child's tastes and peculiarities, in their efforts to instruct and train him. While, however, they are making study attractive and life enjoyable to a child, parents should see to it that the child learns to keep quiet at specified times, and to be active at other times; that he studies assigned lessons, does set tasks, denies himself craved indulgences; that he goes and comes, that he stands or moves, at designated hours, — not because he wants to do these things, but because he *must*. Now, as of old, "It is good for a man that he bear the yoke in his youth."

SEVEN

DENYING A CHILD WISELY

One of the hardest and one of the most important things in the training of a loved child is to deny him that which he longs for, and which we could give to him, but which he would better not have. It is very pleasant to gratify a child. There is real enjoyment in giving to him what he asks for, when we can do it prudently. But wise withholding is quite as important as generous giving in the proper care of a child.

Next to denying a child necessary food and raiment, for the sustenance of very life, the unkindest treatment of a child is to give him everything that he asks for. Every parent recognizes this truth within certain limits, and therefore refuses an unsheathed knife, or a percussion cartridge, or a cup of poison, to a child who cries for it. But the breadth and the full significance of the principle involved are not so generally accepted as they should be.

A child ought to be denied, by his parents, many things which in themselves are harmless. It is an injury to any child to have always at the table the dishes which he likes best; to have uniformly the cut or the portion which he prefers; to have every plaything which his parents can afford to give him; to dress—even within their means—just as he wants to;

and to go, with them, where and when he pleases. That child who has never a legitimate desire ungratified is poorly fitted for the duties and the trials of everyday life in the world. He does not, indeed, enjoy himself now as he might hope to through a different training. It is sadly to a parent's discredit when a child can truly say, "My father, or my mother, never denied me any pleasure which it was fairly in his, or her, power to bestow."

It is because of the evil results of not wisely denying the little ones, that an only child is in so many instances spoken of as a spoiled child. There is but one to give to in that household. He can have just so much more, than if there were half a dozen children to share it; and, as a rule, he gets it all. Parents give to him freely; so do grandparents, and so do uncles and aunts. He hardly knows what self-denial or want is. His very fullness palls upon him. It is not easy to surprise him with an unexpected pleasure. He not only is liable to grow selfish and exacting, but at the best he lacks all the enjoyment which comes of the occasional gratification of a desire which has been long felt without the expectation of its being speedily met.

But it is by no means *necessary* that an only child should be spoiled in training. Some of the best trained children in the world have been only children. Many a parent is more faithful and discreet in securing to his or her only child the benefits of self-denial than is many another with half a dozen children to care for. But whether there be one child or more in the family, the lesson of wise denial is alike important to the young, and the responsibility of its teaching should be recognized by the parent.

Few grown persons can have everything they want, everything that love can give, everything that money can buy. Most of them have many reasonable wishes ungratified, many moderate desires unfilled. They have to get along without a great many things which others have, and which they would like. It is probable that their children will be called to similar experiences when they must finally shift for themselves. Their children ought, therefore, to be in training for this experience now. It is largely the early education which gives one proper control over himself and his desires. If in childhood one is taught to deny himself, to yield gracefully much that he longs for, to enjoy the little that he can have in spite of the lack of a great deal which he would like to have, his lot will be an easier and happier one, when he comes to the realities of maturer life, than would be possible to him if, as a child, he had only to express a reasonable wish, to have it promptly gratified.

For this reason it is that men who were the children of the rich are so often at a disadvantage, in the battle of life, in comparison with those who have risen from comparative poverty. Their parents' wealth, so freely at their disposal, increased the number of wants which they now think must be gratified. Their pampering in childhood so enervated them for the struggles and endurances which are, at the best, a necessity in ordinary business pursuits, that they are easily distanced by those who were in youth disciplined through enforced self-denial, and made strong by enduring hardness, and by finding contentment with a little. It is a great pity that the full and free gifts of a loving parent should prove a hindrance to a child's happiness, a barrier to his success in life; that the very abundance of the parent's giving should tend to the child's poverty and unhappiness! Yet this state of things is in too many instances an undeniable fact.

Children of the present day—especially children of parents in comfortable worldly circumstances—are far more likely than were their fathers and mothers to lack lessons of self-denial. The standard of living is very different now from a generation since. There were few parents in any community in this country fifty years ago who could buy whatever they wanted for their children; or, indeed, for themselves.

There was no such freeness of purchases for children, for the table, for the house or the household, as is now common on every side. Children then did not expect a new suit of clothes every few months. Often they had old ones made over for them, from those of their parents or of their elder brothers and sisters. A present from the toy-shop or book-store was a rarity in those days. There was not much choosing by children what they would eat as they sat down at the family table. There was still less of planning by them for a summer journey with their parents to a mountain or seaside resort. Self-denial, or more or less of personal privation, came as a necessity to almost every child in the younger days of many who are now on the stage of active life. But how different now!

The average child of the present generation receives more presents and more indulgences from his parents in any one year of his life than the average child of a generation ago received in all the years of his childhood. Because of this new standard, the child of today expects new things, as a matter of course; he asks for them, in the belief that he will receive them. In consequence of their abundance, he sets a smaller value upon them severally. It is not possible that he should think as highly of any one new thing, out of a hundred coming to him in rapid succession, as he would of the only gift of an entire year.

A boy of nowadays can hardly prize his new bicycle, or his "double-ripper" sled, after all the other presents he has received, as his father prized a little wagon made of a raisin-box, with wheels of ribbon-blocks, which was *his* only treasure in the line of locomotion. A little girl cannot have as profound enjoyment in her third wax doll of the year, with eyes which open and shut, as her mother had with her one clumsy doll of stuffed rags or of painted wood. A new child's book was a wonder a generation since; it is now hardly more to one of our children than the evening paper is to the father of the family. It is now hard work to give a new sensation—or, at all events, to make a permanent impression—by the bestowal of a gift of any sort on a child. It would be far easier to surprise and to impress many a child by refusing to give to him what he asked for and expected; and that treatment would in some cases be greatly to a child's advantage.

A distinctive feature of the child training of the ancient Spartans was the rigid discipline of constant self-denial, to which the child was subjected from infancy onward. And this feature of child training among that people had much to do with giving to the Spartans their distinguishing characteristics of simplicity of manners, of powers of endurance, and of dauntless bravery. The best primitive peoples everywhere have recognized the pre-eminent importance of this feature of child training. Its neglect has come only with the growth in luxury among peoples of the highest material civilization. The question is an important one, whether it is well to lose all the advantages of this method of training, simply because it is not found to be a necessity as a means of sustaining physical life, where wealth abounds so freely.

It is not that a child is to be denied what he wants, merely for the sake of the denial itself; but it is that a child ought not to have what he wants merely because he wants it. It is not that there is a necessary gain in a denial to a child; but it is that when a denial to a child is necessary, there is an added gain to him through his finding that he must do without what he longs for. It is every parent's duty to deny a child many things which he wants; to teach him that he must get along without a great many things which seem very desirable; to train him to self-denial and endurance, at the table, in the playroom; with companions, and away from them; and the doing of this duty by the parent brings a sure advantage to the child. Whatever else he has, a child ought not lack this element of wise training.

EIGHT

HONORING A CHILD'S INDIVIDUALITY

A child is liable to be looked upon as if he were simply one child among many children, a specimen representative of childhood generally; but every child stands all by himself in the world as an individual, with his own personality and character, with his own thoughts and feelings, his own hopes and fears and possibilities, his own relations to his fellow beings and to God. This truth is often realized by a child before his parents realize it; and if it be unperceived and unrecognized by his parents, they are thereby shut off from the opportunity of doing for him much that can be done by them only as they give due honor to their child's individuality as a child.

A little babe is not a mere bit of child-material, to be worked up by outside efforts and influences into a child-reality; but he is already a living organism, with all the possibilities of his highest manhood working within him toward his independent development. Here is the difference, on a lower plane, between a mass of clay being molded by the sculptor's hands into a statue of grace and beauty, and a seed of herb or tree containing within itself the germ of a new and peculiar individual specimen of its own unchanging species. An acorn is more than the fruit of the oak that bore it; it is the germ of another oak, like, and yet unlike, all the oaks that the world has known before the growth of this one. So, also, a child is more than the mere child of his earthly parents; he is, in embryo, a man with characteristics and qualities such as his parents could never attain to, and which, it may be, the world has never before seen equaled.

The possibilities of Moses, who was to put his impress upon the world's character, were in the Hebrew babe, as his loving mother laid him tenderly in the pitch-daubed basket of papyrus, to hide him away among the flags of the Nile border, as they were not in any native babe of the household of Pharoah; and if his mother had any intuitive womanly sense of his grand future in the providence of God, her zeal and faith in his behalf were quickened and inspired accordingly. And so it has been all along the ages; the germs of power and achievement were already in the babe, who was afterward known as Plato, or Caesar, or Mohammad, or Charlemagne, or Columbus, or Shakespeare, or Washington. And who will doubt that many a germ of such possibility in a young child has been quickened or repressed, according as that child's parents have perceived and honored, or have failed to realize and to foster, the best that was involved in the child's individuality?

It was to the credit of the high priest Eli, that he perceived that the child Samuel was capable of receiving communications from the Lord, such as were denied to the possessor of Urim and Thummim; and that he honored the child's individuality so far as to encourage him to declare the message that God had sent by him; instead of treating the child as one who could receive nothing from God, save as it came to him through the medium of his guardians and seniors. This spirit it was that prompted Trebonius to bare his head as he entered the school-room where he was looked up to as the teacher; because, as he suggested, he recognized in every child before him there the possibility of lofty attainment in his developed individuality. And it can hardly be doubted that this attitude of the teacher Trebonius had its measure of influence in bringing to its fruition the germinal power in his pupil Martin Luther. Trebonius and Eli are—so far, at least—a pattern to the parents of today.

It is not merely that the child *is to be* the possessor of a marked and distinctive individuality, and that therefore he is to be honored for his possibilities in that direction; but it is that *he already is* the possessor of such an individuality, and that he is worthy of honor for that which he has and is at the present time. Many a child, while a child, is the superior of his parents in the basis and scope of character, in the attributes of genius, and in the instincts of high spiritual perception. This is the true order of things in the progress of God's plans for the race; the better is in the coming generations, not in the past. But even where the child is not the superior, he is always the peer in individuality of those to whom he looks up with honoring reverence as his parents, and he is entitled to recognition by them in that peership.

Everyone who recalls clearly his childhood thoughts and feelings, remembers that even in his earliest days he had his own standpoint of observation and reflection; that he was conscious of his individual relations to others and to God; and that, in a sense, his independent outlook and his independent uplook as an individual were the same then as now, in kind, although not in degree. He also remembers that, as a child, he was often made to feel that his individuality was not fully recognized by others, but that it was frequently ignored or trenched upon by those who took it for granted that, because he was still a child, he had as yet no truly individual position, attitude, and rights in the world. Yet it is not an easy thing for a parent of today to bear always in mind that every child of his is as truly an individual as he was when he was a child.

In little things, as in larger, a child's individuality is liable to be overlooked, or to be disregarded. A little boy was taken alarmingly ill one day. For several hours his loving mother watched him anxiously. The next day he was in his accustomed health again. His mother, with the evident thought that a child could have no comprehension like a parent's of such a state of things as that, said to him, tenderly: "My dear boy, you don't know how sick you were yesterday." "Oh, yes! I do, dear mamma," he answered; "I know a great deal better than you do; for I was the one that was sick." And many a child has the thought that was in that child's mind, when he is spoken to as though he must get all his ideas of his own feelings and conditions and needs from someone who is supposed to represent him better than he can represent himself—while he is still in childhood.

It is much the same in the matter of personal rights, as in the matter of personal feelings. A child finds that his individuality is constantly lost sight of, because he is a child; as it ought not to be. A little fellow who had been given a real watch, was conscious of an advance in his relative position by that possession. His uncle, having taken his own watch to the watchmaker's, asked the loan of the little fellow's watch for the time being, saying that he could not get along without one. "Can't you get along without a watch?" asked the nephew. "No, I cannot," replied the uncle. "If I had mine at the watchmaker's, would you lend me yours till mine came back?" was the little fellow's searching inquiry. "Why, no; I don't suppose I would," replied the other. "But then, you know, I'm a man, and you are a boy." "Well, then," said the individual boy to the individual man; "if you can't get along without a watch, and you wouldn't lend me yours if I needed it, I can't get along without a watch, and I can't let you have mine."

Now, the trouble in that case was that the boy's individuality was not sufficiently recognized and honored by the manner of that request for his watch. It seemed to be taken for granted that, because he was a child, he had no such rights to his own possessions as a man has to his, and that he put no such value on that which he had, as a man would be sure to put on his belongings. Against that assumption the child quite naturally, and with a good show of logic, resolutely asserted himself. If, on the other hand, the boy had been appealed to as an equal, to render a favor to the other because of a special and a clearly explained need, there is no reason to doubt that he would have been prompt to respond to it, with a feeling of satisfaction in being able to render that favor.

Just here is where so many children are deprived of their rights as individuals, by inconsiderate parents or others. When seats are lacking for new comers in a room or a street-car, and two or three children are seated together by themselves in absorbing chat, the temptation is to speak quickly to the little ones, telling them to vacate those seats for their elders, in a tone that seems to indicate that a child has no rights in comparison with a grown person; instead of showing by the very manner of address that the children's attention is called to their privilege of showing courtesy to their elders. In the one case, every child of that party feels aggrieved through being made to feel that his rights are not recognized as rights. In the other case, he is gratified by the implied confidence in his gentlemanliness, and in his readiness to yield his rights gracefully. A child's rights as an individual are as positive and as sacred as a man's; and it is never proper to ignore these rights in a child, anymore than it would be in a man.

When a child shows an unexpected interest in a subject of conversation between adults, it is not fair for the adults to brush aside the child's questions or comments in a way that seems to say, "Oh! you are only a child. Your opinions are of no account. This is a matter for real people to think and talk about." Yet how common a thing it is for parents to treat their children in this way; and what a mistake it is! If, indeed, the subject be one that is fairly beyond a child's grasp, it is quite proper to give the child to understand this fact, without any lack of respect for his individuality; but under no circumstances is it right to ignore that individuality at such a time.

The deeper the theme of converse, and the profounder the thought involved in it, the greater the probability of a child's freshness and life in its considering, if he indicates an appreciative interest in its discussion. It is not merely in the story of the child Samuel that there is a gleam of childhood's possibilities in the direction of closer communion with God than is granted to ordinary manhood; but all the teachings of Scripture and of human experience tend to the disclosure and confirmation of this same truth. "Verily I say unto you," says our Lord, "Except ye turn, and become as little children, ye shall in no wise enter into the kingdom of heaven." And again: "See that ye despise not one of these little ones; for I say unto you, that in heaven their angels do always behold the face of my Father which is in heaven." And there is an echo of these Divine words in the familiar teachings of the Christian poet of nature:

Heaven lies about us in our infancy!
Shades of the prison-house begin to close
    Upon the growing Boy,
But he beholds the light, and whence it flows, —
    He sees it in his joy;
The Youth, who daily farther from the East
Must travel, still is Nature's priest,
    And by the vision splendid
    Is on his way attended;
At length the Man perceives it die away,
And fade into the light of common day.

There is, indeed, a possibility of retaining the child-freshness of acquaintance with spiritual truths even into manhood and through all one's life. That possibility every parent ought to strive to attain to. "Whosoever therefore shall humble himself as this little child," said our Lord, as he pointed to a veritable human little one, "the same is the greatest in the kingdom of heaven." And he who is greatest through being most childlike, will be readiest to recognize the individuality and the glorious possibilities of each and every child committed to his charge. Even while training a child, he will learn from the child; and so he and his child will grow together toward the measure of the stature of the fullness of Christ.

LETTING ALONE AS A MEANS OF CHILD TRAINING

Not doing is always as important, in its time and place, as doing; and this truth is as applicable in the realm of child training as elsewhere. Child training is a necessity, but there is a danger of overdoing in the line of child training. The neglect of child training is a great evil. Overdoing in the training of a child may be even a greater evil. Both evils ought to be avoided. In order to their avoidance, their existence and limits as evils must be recognized.

Peculiarly is it the case that young parents who are exceptionally conscientious, and exceptionally desirous of being wise and faithful in the discharge of their parental duties, are liable to err in the direction of overdoing in the training of their children. It is not that they are lacking in love and tenderness toward their little ones, or that they are naturally inclined to severity as disciplinarian; but it is that their mistaken view of the methods and limitations of wise child training impels them to an injudicious course of watchful strictness with their children, even while that course runs counter to their affections and desires as parents. Their very love and fidelity cause them to harm their children by overdoing in their training, even more than the children of parents less wise and faithful are harmed by a lack of systematic training. It is, in fact, because they are so desirous of welldoing, that these parents overdo in the line of their best endeavors for their children.

A young father who was an earnest student of methods of child training, and who sincerely desired to be faithful in the training of his first child at any cost to his feelings of loving tenderness toward that child, made a mistake in this direction, and received a lesson accordingly. His child was as full of affection as she was of life and spirit. She had not yet learned what she might do and what she might not do, but she was rapidly developing impulses and tastes in various directions; and her strength of personal character was showing itself in her positiveness of purpose in the line of her tastes and impulses for the hour. Her father had heard much about the importance of parental training and discipline, but had heard nothing about the danger of overdoing in this line; hence he deemed it his duty to be constantly directing or checking his child, so as to keep her within the limits of safety and duty as he saw it.

To his surprise and regret, the father found that, while his little daughter was not inclined to waywardness or disobedience, she was steadily coming into a state of chronic resistance to his attempts at her stricter governing. This resistance was passive rather than active, but it was none the less real for that. She would not refuse to obey, but she would not be ready or prompt to obey. She would not be aroused to anger or show any open sign of disrespect, but she would seem unable or unwilling to act as she was told to. Kind words and earnest entreaties were of no avail at this point, neither were they resented or explicitly rejected. If punishment was attempted, she submitted to it with a good grace, but it seemed to have no effect in the way of removing the cause of original trouble. The father never, indeed, lost his temper, or grew less loving toward his child; he prayed for guidance, and he gave his best thoughts to the problem before him; but all to no apparent purpose. The matter grew more and more serious, and he was more and more bewildered.

One day, after a serious struggle with his little daughter over a matter that would have been a trifling one except as it bore on the question of her character and welfare, the father left his house with a heavy heart, and almost in despair over this question of wise child training. At the door he met a friend, much older than himself, with whom he had been a co-worker in several spheres of Christian activity. Seeing his troubled face, that friend asked him the cause of his evident anxiety, and the young father opened his heart, and told the story of his trouble. "Isn't the trouble, that you are overdoing in the training of your child?" asked the listener; and then he went on to give his own experience in illustration of the meaning of this question.

"My first child was my best child," he said; "and I harmed her for life by overdoing in her training, as I now see, in looking back over my course with her. I thought I must be training her all the time, and I forced issues with her, and took notice of little things, when I would have done better to let her alone. So she was checked unduly, and shut up within herself by my course with her; and she grew up in a rigid and unnatural constraint which ought not to have been hers. I saw my mistake afterwards, and I allowed my other children more freedom, by letting them alone except when they must be interfered with; and I've seen the benefit of this course. My rule with all my children, since my first, has been to avoid an issue with them on a question of discipline whenever I could do so safely. And the less show of training there is, in bringing up a child, the better, as I see it."

This was a revelation to that young father. He determined at once to try to act on its suggestions, since the opposite course had been such a signal failure in his hands. When again in his home, an opportunity for an experiment was soon before him. His little daughter came into the room, through a door which she had been repeatedly told to push to, after she had passed it. Without any special thought on the subject, the father, who sat writing at his desk, said, as often before: "Push the door to, darling." And, as often before, the child stood quiet and firm, as if in expectation of a new issue on that point. The counsel of the morning came into the father's mind, and he said gently, "You needn't shut the door to, darling, if you don't want to. Papa will do it," and at once he stepped and closed the door, returning afterwards to his desk, without a word of rebuke to his child.

This was a new experience to the poor overtaxed child. She stood in perplexed thought for a few minutes. Then she came lovingly to her father, and, asking to be taken up on his knee, she clasped her arms about his neck, and said: "Dear papa, I'm sorry I didn't shut that door. I will next time. Please forgive me, dear papa." And that was the beginning of a new state of things in that home. The father had learned that there was a danger of overdoing in the work of child training, and his children were afterwards the gainers by his added knowledge of the needs and tastes of childhood.

In the case of this father, the trouble had been that he made too many direct issues with his child on questions of authority and obedience, and that thus he provoked conflicts which might have been wisely avoided. After this new experience he was very cautious at this point, and he soon found that his child could be trained to obey without so often considering the possibility of resisting or questioning parental authority. When, in any case, an issue had to be accepted, the circumstances were so well considered that the child as well as the parent saw that its right outcome was the only outcome. The error of this father had been the error of a thoughtful and deliberate disciplinarian, who was as yet but partially instructed; but there are also thoughtless and inconsiderate parents who harm, if they do not ruin, their children's dispositions by overdoing in what they call child training. And this error is even worse than the other.

There are many parents who seem to suppose that their chief work in the training of a child is to be incessantly commanding and prohibiting; telling the child to do this or to do that, and not to do this, that, or the other. But this nagging a child is not training a child; on the contrary, it is destructive of all training on the part of him who is addicted to it. It is not the driver who is training a horse, but one who neither is trained nor can train, who is all the time "yanking" at the reins, or "thrapping" them up and down. Neither parent nor driver, in such a case, can do as much in the direction of training by doing incessantly, as by letting alone judiciously. "Don't be always don't-ing," is a bit of counsel to parents that can hardly be emphasized too strongly. Don't be always directing, in a companion precept to this. Both injunctions are needful, with the tendency of human nature as it is.

Of course, there must be explicit commanding and explicit prohibiting in the process of child training; but there must also be a large measure of wise letting alone. When to prohibit and when to command, in this process, are questions that demand wisdom, thought, and character; and more wisdom, more thought, and more character, are needful in deciding the question when to let the child alone. The training of a child must go on incessantly; but a large share of the time it will best go on by the operation of influences, inspirations, and inducements, in the direction of a right standard held persistently before the child, without anything being said on the subject to the child at every step in his course of progress. Doing nothing, as a child-trainer, is, in its order, the best kind of doing.

TEN

TRAINING A CHILD
TO SELF-CONTROL

An inevitable struggle between the individual and the several powers that go to make his individuality, begins in every child at his very birth, and continues so long as his life in the flesh continues. On the outcome of this struggle depends the ultimate character of him who struggles. It is, to him, bondage or mastery, defeat or triumph, failure or success, as a result of the battling that cannot be evaded. And, as a matter of fact, the issue of the lifelong battle is ordinarily settled in childhood.

A child who is trained to self-control — as a child may be — is already a true man in his fitness for manly self-mastery. A man who was not trained, in childhood, to self-control, is hopelessly a child in his combat with himself; and he can never regain the vantage-ground which his childhood gave him, in the battle which then opened before him, and in the thick of which he still finds himself. It is in a child's earlier struggles with himself that help can easiest be given to him, and that it is of greatest value for his own developing of character. Yet at that time a child has no such sense of his need in this direction as is sure to be his in maturer years; hence it is that it rests with the parent to decide, while the child is still a child, whether the child shall be a slave to himself, or a master of himself; whether his life, so far, shall be worthy or unworthy of his high possibilities of manhood.

A child's first struggle with himself ought to be in the direction of controlling his impulse to give full play to his lungs and his muscles at the prompting of his nerves. As soon as the nerves make themselves felt, they prompt a child to cry, to thrash his arms, to kick, and to twist his body on every side, at the slightest provocation—or at none. Unless this prompting be checked, the child will exhaust himself in aimless exertion, and will increase his own discomfort by the very means of its exhibit. A control of himself at this point is possible to a child, at an age while he is yet unable to speak, or to understand what is spoken to him. If a parent realizes that the child *must* be induced to control himself, and seeks in loving firmness to cause the child to realize that same truth, the child will *feel* the parent's conviction, and will yield to it, even though he cannot comprehend the meaning of his parent's words as words. The way of helping the child will be found, by the parent who wills to help him. To leave a child to himself in these earliest struggles with himself, is to put him at a sad disadvantage in all the future combats of his life's warfare; while to give him wise help in these earliest struggles, is to give him help for all the following struggles.

As soon as a child is able to understand what is said to him, he ought to be taught and trained to control his impulse to cry and writhe under the pressure of physical pain. When a child has fallen and hurt himself, or has cut his finger, or has burned his hand, or has been hit by an ill-directed missile, it is natural for him to shriek with pain and fright, and it is natural for his tender-hearted mother to shrink from blaming him just then for indulging in this display of grief. But even at such a time as this, a mother has an unmistakable duty of helping her child to gain a measure of control over himself, so as to repress his cries and to moderate his exhibit of disturbed feeling.

A child can come to exercise self-control under such circumstances as these. His mother can enable him to do this. It is better for both child and mother that he should have her help accordingly. Because of the lack of help just here, many a child is a sufferer through life in his inability to control himself under physical pain. And because of this inability many a person has actually lost his life, at a time when calmness of mind was essential to that endurance of physical suffering which was the only hope of prolonged existence. Because he was not trained to control his nerves, he is hopelessly controlled by his nerves.

Coaxing and rewarding a child into quiet at such a time is not what is needed; but it is the encouraging a child into an intelligent control of himself, that is to be aimed at by the wise parent. It is only a choice between evils that substitutes a candy-paid silence for a noisy indulgence of feeling on a child's part. A good illustration of the unwise way of inducing children to seem to have control of themselves, is given in the familiar story of the little fellow throwing himself on the floor and kicking and yelling, and then crying out, "Grandma, grandma, I want to be pacified. Where are your sugar-plums?"

Dr. Bushnell, protesting against this method of coaxing a child out of a state of irritation, in a fit of ill-nature, by "dainties that please the taste," says forcefully, "It must be a very dull child that will not cry and fret a great deal, when it is so pleasantly rewarded. Trained, in this manner, to play ill-nature for sensation's sake, it will go on rapidly, in the course of double attainment, and will be very soon perfected in the double character of an ill-natured, morbid sensualist, and a feigning cheat besides. By what methods, or means, can the great themes of God and religion get hold of a soul that has learned to be governed only by rewards of sensation, paid to affectations of grief and deliberate actings of ill-nature?"

That control of himself which is secured by a child in his intelligent repression of an impulse to cry and writhe in physical pain, is of advantage to the child in all his lifelong struggle with himself; and he should be trained in the habit of making his self-control available to him in this struggle. "I buffet my body [or give it a black eye] and bring it into bondage; lest by any means, after that I have preached to others, I myself should be rejected," says the Apostle Paul; as if in recognition of the fact that a man's battle with his body is a vital conflict, all his life through. Every child needs the help of his parents in gaining control over his body, instead of allowing his body to gain the control of him. The appetites and passions and impellings of the outer man are continually striving for the mastery over the inner man; and unless one is trained to master these instead of being mastered by them, he is sure to fail in his life struggle.

A parent ought to help his child to refrain from laughing when he ought not to laugh; from crying when he ought not to cry; from speaking when he ought not to speak; from eating that which he ought not to eat, even though the food be immediately before him; from running about when it is better for him to remain quiet; and to be ready to say and to do just that which it is best for him to say and do, at the time when it needs to be said and done. Self-control in all these things is possible to a child. Wise training on the parent's part can secure it. The principle which is operative here, is operative in every sphere of human existence. By means of self-control a child is made happier, and is fitted for his duties, while a child and ever after, as otherwise he could not be. Many a man's lifecourse is saddened through his hopeless lack of that self-control to which he could easily have been helped in childhood, if only his parents had understood his needs and been faithful accordingly.

ELEVEN

TRAINING A CHILD NOT TO TEASE

A child who never "teases" is a rarity; yet no child ought to tease. If a child does tease, the blame of his teasing properly rests on his parents, rather than on himself. The parent who realizes this fact, will have an added stimulus to the work of training his child not to tease; and no phase of the work of child training is simpler, or surer of its result, than this one.

"To tease" is "to pull," "to tug," "to drag," "to vex [or carry] with importunity." A child teases when he wants something from his parents, and fails to get it at the first asking. He pulls and tugs at his parents, in the hope of dragging them to his way of thinking, or to a consent to his having what he wants in spite of their different thinking. He hopes to vex or carry them into the line of his desires by means of his importunities, whatever their view of the case may have been to begin with. If a child could have what he wanted at his first asking, he would not tease; for there would be no room for his teasing. If a child never secured anything through teasing, he would not come into the habit of teasing; for there would be no inducement to him to tease. When, therefore, a child is accustomed to tease, it is evident that he has been trained by his parents to tease, instead of being trained by them not to tease; and they are to bear the responsibility and blame of his teasing.

Many a child does not expect to get what he wants, if it is out of the ordinary line of his daily needs, unless he teases for it; therefore he counts teasing a part of his regular duty in life, as truly as "beating down" the city shopkeeper on his prices is supposed to be the duty of the shopper from the country. If a child asks for a slice of bread and butter, or a bit of meat, at the family table, or for a glass of water between meals, he expects to get it at the first asking. Teasing for that is not in his mind as a necessity. But if he wants to stay at home from school without any reason for it, or to start off with some of his schoolmates on a long and hazardous tramp on a Saturday, or to sit up an hour later than usual at night, or to have a new sled or velocipede or bicycle, or to go to the circus or to hear the minstrels, "like all the other fellows"—he is not so sure of gaining his request at the first asking. So, when the answer "No" comes back to him, in such a case, he meets it with the appeal, "Do let me. Oh, do!" and then he enters upon a nerve struggle for the mastery over his parents at this point, with the idea in his mind that it is a single question of who shall be most persistent in adhering to his side of the conflict.

There are few children who always succeed in carrying their point by teasing; but there are fewer who never succeed by this means. Most parents give way, sooner or later, in some of these conflicts with their children. It may be that they are less determined than their children, and that they are simply tired out by the teasing. It may be that they are moved by their children's earnestness in the matter, and that they yield because of their tenderness toward the little pleaders. It may be that their first answer to the appeal is a thoughtless one, and that their fuller considering of the matter leads them to see it to be right to reverse their impulsive decision. Whatever be the parents' reason for their course in such a case, if they give a negative answer to their children's first request, and an affirmative one in response to more or less teasing on the children's part, they train their children so far to believe that teasing is an important factor in a child's progress in life; and of course they are responsible for their children's continuance in the habit of teasing.

It is a misfortune to a child to suppose that teasing is essential to his gaining a point that he ought to gain. A result of such a view in his mind is, that he looks not to his parents' wisdom and judgment, but to his own positiveness and persistency, as the guide of his action in any mooted case of personal conduct; not to principles which are disclosed to him by one who is in authority, but to impulses which are wholly in his own bosom. Such a view is inimical to all wise methods of thinking and doing on a child's part. And it is even more of a misfortune to the parent than to the child, for a child to have the idea that the parent's decision is a result of the child's teasing, rather than of the parent's understanding of what is right and best in a given case. No parent can have the truest respect of a child, while the child knows that he can tease that parent into compliance with the child's request, contrary to the parent's real or supposed conviction. For the child's sake, therefore, and also for the parent's, every child ought to be trained not to tease, and not to expect any possible advantage from teasing.

Susannah Wesley, the mother of John and Charles Wesley, was accustomed to say, of her children, that they all learned very early that they were not to have anything that they cried for, and that so they soon learned not to cry for a thing that they wanted. Who will doubt that John and Charles Wesley were stronger men, for this training, than they could have been if they were trained to look upon crying as a means of securing what was best for them? Who will doubt that Susannah Wesley was more of a woman, and

more respected by her sons because of her unvarying firmness at this point, than would have been possible if she had
frequently yielded to the pressure of their piteous crying for
that which it was against her judgment to give to them? Any
parent who would apply this rule of Susannah Wesley to the
matter of teasing, might be sure of a corresponding result in
the children's estimate of the practical value of teasing. Any
child who finds that he is never to have anything for which
he teases, will quickly quit teasing. How simple this rule, for
this department of child training!

Simple as it seems, however, to be uniformly positive in
refusing to give to a child anything for which he teases, it is
not an easy thing to adhere to this rule, unvaryingly, and to
do it wisely. And the trouble in the case is not with the
child, but with the parent. In order to give promptly, to a
child's request, an answer that can rightly be insisted upon
against all entreaties, a parent must do his thinking before
he gives that answer, rather than afterwards. Too often a
parent denies a child's request at the start without considering the case in all its bearings; and then, when the child
presses his suit, the parent sees reasons for granting it which
had not been in his mind before. The child perceives this
state of things, and realizes that the question is to be settled
by his teasing, rather than by his parent's independent judgment; and that, therefore, teasing is the only means of
securing a correct decision in the premises.

Training a child not to tease, is a duty incumbent upon
every parent; but, as a prerequisite to this training of the
child, the parent must himself be trained. When a child asks
a favor of a parent, the parent must not reply hastily, or
thoughtlessly, or without a full understanding of the case in
all its involvings. If necessary, he may question the child, in
order to a better understanding of the case, or he may postpone his answer until he can learn more about it; but he
must not be over quick to reply merely as a means of push-

ing away the request for the time being. He must consider carefully what his final answer ought to be, before he gives an answer that the child is to accept as final; and when the parent gives that answer, it ought to be with such kindly firmness that the child will not think of pressing his suit by teasing. And thus it is that any well-trained parent can train his child well in this sphere.

TWELVE

TRAINING A CHILD'S APPETITE

What a grown person likes to eat or drink depends largely on what that person was trained to eat or drink while a child. And a child can be trained to like almost any sort of food or drink, either good or bad. No small responsibility, therefore, for both the health and the enjoyment of a child, devolves on him who has in hand the training of a child's appetite.

That a child inherits tastes in the matter of food and drink cannot be questioned; but this fact does not forbid the training of a child's tastes away from its inborn tendencies; it merely adds an element to be considered in the training process. A child born in the tropics soon learns to like the luscious fruits which are given to him freely; while a child born in the arctic regions learns with the same rapidity to like the grosser diet of fish and oil which is his chief supply of food. In one region the people live mainly on roots and berries; in another, they devour raw flesh or drink fresh blood; in yet another, they eat dried locusts or grasshoppers; in yet another, it is milk or honey which is their chief means of sustaining life. In every region the children are easily trained to enjoy the eating of that which they have to eat;

and if a child is taken at an early age from one region to another, he quickly adapts himself to his new conditions, and learns to like that which is given to him as his means of satisfying hunger. All of which goes to show that the natural appetite of a child does not demand one kind of food above another, to that extent which forbids the training of a child to enjoy that which he can have and which he ought to use.

As a rule, very little attention is given to the training of a child's appetite. The child is supplied with that food which is easiest obtained, and which the child is readiest to take. If the parents give little thought to their children's welfare, they simply allow their children to share with them at the common table, without considering whether or not the food is that which is best suited to the children's needs. If the parents are tenderhearted, and lovingly indulgent toward their children, they are quite likely to show favor by giving to them those things which please a child's palate, or which are favorites with the parents themselves.

Finding that a child likes sugar, a parent is tempted to give a bit of sugar to a child who is not ready to take anything else at its mealtime; even though that bit of sugar may destroy the child's appetite for the hour, or disturb the child's stomach for all day. Again, seeing that the child is glad to try any article of food which his parent enjoys, the parent, perhaps, proffers from his own plate that which he deems a delicacy; although it may be of all things the least suited to the child's state of health, or condition of being. And so it is that the child is trained in wrong ways of eating, at the very time when he most needs training in the right way.

A child is quite likely to have his freaks and fancies of appetite, which a kind parent is tempted to indulge instead of checking. One child would eat only the softer part of bread, while rejecting its crust. One would eat meat without vegetables; another would refuse one kind of meat, or of vegetables, while eating all others freely; and so on. The more these peculiarities are indulged, the stronger becomes their hold on the child. The more they are checked and restrained, the weaker their power becomes. Yet most parents seem to count such peculiarities as beyond their control, and therefore to be accepted as inevitable; instead of realizing their personal responsibility for the continuance or the removal of them.

"Your boy ought to eat less meat and more farinaceous food," says a physician to a mother, whose boy is in the doctor's hands. "Let him have oatmeal and milk for breakfast; and see to it that he eats meat only once a day, and sparingly at that." "Johnny is a great hand for meat," is the answer; "and he can't take oatmeal." And in that answer the mother shows that all the blame in the case rests on herself, and not on her Johnny. Johnny ought to have been trained to eat what is good for him, instead of indulging his personal whims in the eating line.

When a mother says, "My boy won't eat potatoes," or "He won't eat tomatoes," or "He will eat no meat but beef," she simply confesses to her culpable failure of duty in the training of her boy's appetite. If she were to say that she did not approve of one of those things, or of the other, and therefore she would not give it to him, that would be one thing; but when she says that he will not take it even though she thinks it best for him, that is quite another thing; and there is where the blame comes in.

Of course, it is to be understood that there are articles of food in familiar use which, here and there, a child cannot eat with safety. On the seashore, for example, the clam, which is eaten freely by most persons, seems to be as poison to certain individuals. It is not that these persons do not like the clam; but it is that their systems recoil from it, and that its eating is sure to bring on a serious illness. A like state of things exists with regard to fresh strawberries in the country. They are a delicious fruit in the estimation of most persons. They are as a mild form of poison to certain individuals. But these cases are abnormal ones. They have no practical bearing on the prevailing rule, that a child can be trained to like whatever he ought to eat, and to refrain from the eating of whatever is not best for him. And herein is the principle of wise training in the realm of a child's appetite.

A prominent American educator put this principle into practice in his own family, consisting of four boys and four girls. He was a man of limited means, and he felt the necessity of training his children to eat such food as he deemed proper for them, and as good as he could afford to supply. His choice of food for his family table was wisely made, to begin with; and then he showed wisdom in his mode of pressing it upon his children.

If those children deemed a dish distasteful, they were privileged to wait until they were willing to eat it. There was no undue pressure brought to bear on them. They could simply eat it, or let it alone. If they went without it that meal, the same dish, or a similar one, was before them for the next meal; and so on until hunger gave them the zest to eat it with unfeigned heartiness. By this means those children learned to eat what they ought to eat; and when they had come to years of maturity they realized the value of this training, which had made them the rulers of their appetite, instead of being its slaves. It needs no single example to illustrate the opposite course from this one. On every side we see persons who are subject to the whims and caprices of their appetite, because their appetite was never trained to be subject to them. And in one or another of these two directions the upbringing of every child is tending today.

Peculiarly in the use of candy and of condiments is a child's appetite likely to be untrained, or trained amiss. Neither the one nor the other of these articles is suited to a child's needs; but both of them are allowed to a child, regardless of what is best for him. The candy is given because the child fancies it. The condiments are given because the parents fancy them. Neither of the two is supposed to be beneficial to the child, but each is given in its turn because of the child's wish for it, and of the parent's weakness. There *are* parents who train their children not to eat candy between meals, nor to use condiments at meals. These parents are wiser than the average; and their children are both healthier and happier. There ought to be more of such parents, and more of such children. The difficulty in the way is always with the parents, instead of with the children.

It is affirmed as a fact, that some Shetland ponies which were brought to America had been accustomed to eat fish, and that for a time they refused to eat hay, but finally were trained to its eating until they seemed to enjoy it as heartily as other ponies. Children to whom cod-liver oil was most distasteful when it was first given to them as a medicine, have been trained to like cod-liver oil as well as they liked syrup. And so it has been in the use of acid drinks, or of bitter coffee, by young children under the direction of a physician. By firm and persistent training the children have been brought to like that from which for a time they recoiled. It is for the parents to decide, with the help of a good medical counsel, what their children ought to like, and then to train them to like it.

It is by no means an easy matter for a parent to train a child's appetite; but it is a very important matter, nevertheless. Nothing that is worth doing in this world is an easy matter; and whatever is really worth doing is worth all that its doing costs — and more. In spite of all its difficulties, the training of any child's appetite can be compassed, by God's blessing. And compassed it ought to be, whatever are its difficulties. It is for the parent to decide what the child shall eat, as it is for the parent to decide what the child shall wear. The parent who holds himself responsible for what a child shall put on, but who shirks his responsibility for what that child shall take in, would seem to have more regard for the child's appearances than for his upbuilding from within; and that could hardly be counted a sign of parental wisdom or of parental love.

TRAINING A CHILD AS A QUESTIONER

A child is a born questioner. He does not have to be trained to be a questioner; but he does need to be trained as a questioner. A child has been not inaptly called "an animated interrogation point." Before a child can speak his questions, he looks them; and when he can speak them out, his questions crowd one another for expression, until it would seem that, if a parent were to answer all of his child's questions, that parent would have time to do nothing else. The temptation to a parent, in view of this state of things, is to repress a child as a questioner, rather than to train him as a questioner; and just here is where a parent may lose or undervalue a golden privilege as a parent.

The beginning of all knowledge is a question. All progress in knowledge is a result of continued questioning. Whence? What? Why? Wherefore? Whither? These are the starting-points of investigation and research to young and to old alike; and when any one of these questions has been answered in one sphere, it presents itself anew in another. Unless a child were a questioner at the beginning of his life, he could make no start in knowledge; and if a child were ever caused to stay his questionings, there would be at once

an end to his progress in knowledge. Questioning is the expression of mental appetite. He who lacks the desire to question, is in danger of death from intellectual starvation.

Yet with all the importance that, on the face of it, at-
taches to a child's impulse to ask questions, it is unmistakably true that far more pains are taken by parents
generally to check children in their questionings, than to
train them in their questioning. "Don't be asking so many
questions"; "Why will you be asking questions all the time?"
"You'll worry my life out with your questions." These are the
parental comments on a child's questions, rather than, "I'm
glad to have you want to know about all these things"; or,
"Never hesitate to ask me a question about anything that
you want to know more of"; or, "The more questions you
ask, the better, if only they are proper questions."

Sooner or later the average child comes to feel that, the
fewer questions he asks, the more of a man he will be; and
so he represses his impulse to inquire into the nature and
purpose and meaning of that which newly interests him; until, perhaps, he is no longer curious concerning that which
he does not understand, or is hopeless of any satisfaction
being given to him concerning the many problems which
perplex his wondering mind. By the time he has reached
young manhood, he who was full of questions in order that
he might have knowledge, seems to be willing to live and die
in ignorance, rather than to make a spectacle of himself by
multiplying questions that may be an annoyance to others,
or that may be deemed a source of discredit to himself.

There are obvious reasons why the average parent is not
inclined to encourage his child to ask all the questions he
thinks of. In the first place, it takes a great deal of time to
answer a child's questions. It takes time to feed a child, and
to wash it and dress it; but it takes still more time to supply
food and clothing for a child's mind. And when a parent
finds that the answering of fifty questions in succession from

a child only seems to prompt the child to ask five hundred questions more, it is hardly to be wondered at that the parent thinks there ought to be a stop put to this sort of thing somewhere. Then, again, a child's questions are not always easy to be answered by the child's parent. The average child can ask questions that the average parent cannot answer; and it is not pleasant for a parent to be compelled to confess ignorance on a subject in which his child has a living interest. It is so much easier, and so much more imposing, for a parent to talk to a child on a subject which the parent does understand, and which the child does not, than it is for the parent to be questioned by the child on a subject which neither child nor parent understands, that the parent's temptation is a strong one to discountenance a habit that has this dangerous tendency.

That there ought to be limitations to a child's privilege of question-asking is evident; for every privilege, like every duty, has its limitations. But the limitations of this privilege ought to be as to the time when questions may be asked, and as to the persons of whom they may be asked, rather than as to the extent of the questioning. A child ought not to be free to ask his mother's guest how old she is, or why she does not look as pleasant as his mother; nor yet to ask one of his poorer playmates why he has no better shoes, or how it is that his mother has to do her own washing. A child must not interrupt others in order to ask a question that fills his mind, nor is it always right for him to ask a question of his father or mother before others. When to ask, and of whom to ask, the questions that it is proper for him to ask, must be made known to a child in connection with his training by his parents as a questioner.

It is to the parent that a child ought to be privileged to come in unrestrained freeness as a questioner. Both the mother and the father should welcome from a child any question that the child honestly desires an answer to. And every parent ought to set apart times for a child's free questioning, when the child can feel that the hour is as sacred to that purpose as the hour of morning and evening devotion is sacred to prayer. It may be just before breakfast, or just after, or at the close of the day, that the father is to be always ready to answer his child's special questions. It may be when father and child walk out together, or during the quieter hours of Sunday, that the child is sure of his time for questioning his father. The mother's surest time for helping her child as a questioner, is at the child's bedtime; although her child may be free to sit by her side when she is sewing, or to stand near her when she is busy about other household matters, and to question her while she is thus working. Whenever the child's hour for questioning his parent has come, the child ought to be encouraged to ask any and every question that he really wants to ask; and the parent ought to feel bound to give to the child's every question a loving and well-considered answer.

A child needs parental help in his training as a questioner. While he is to be free to ask questions, he is to exercise his freedom within the limits of reason and of a right purpose. A child may be inclined to multiply silly questions, thoughtless questions, aimless questions. In such a case, he needs to be reminded of his duty of seeking knowledge and of trying to gain it, and that neither his time nor his parent's time ought to be wasted in attending to questions that have no point to them. Again, a child may be inclined to dwell unduly on a single point in his questioning. Then it is his parent's duty to turn him away from that point by inducing him to question on another point. Whenever a child is questioning his parent, that parent has the responsibility and the power of training the child as a questioner, by receiving in kindness and by shaping with discretion the child's commendable impulse and purpose of questioning.

When a child asks a question that a parent really cannot answer, it is a great deal better for the parent to say frankly,

"I do not know," than to say impatiently, "Oh! don't be asking such foolish questions." But, on the other hand, it is often better to give a simple answer, an answer to one point in the child's question, than to attempt an answer that is beyond the child's comprehension, or than to say that it is impossible to explain that subject to a child just now. For example, if a child asks why it is that the sunrise is always to be seen from the windows on one side of the house, and the sunset from the windows on the other side, there is no need of telling him that he is too young to have that explained to him, nor yet of attempting an explanation of the astronomical facts involved. The better is to answer him that the one window looks toward the east and the other toward the west; and that the sun rises in the east and sets in the west. This will give the child one new item of knowledge; and that is all that he cares for just then.

A child may ask a question on a point that cannot with propriety be made clear to him just yet. In such a case he ought not to be rebuked for seeking light, but an answer of some kind is to be given to him, in declaration of a general truth that includes the specific subject of his inquiry, and then he is to be kindly told that by and by he can know more about this than he can now. This will satisfy a well-disposed child for the time being, while it will encourage him to continue in the attitude of a truth-seeking questioner.

A very simple answer to his every question is all that a child looks for; but that is his right, if he is honestly seeking information, and it is his parent's duty to give it to him, if he comes for it at a proper time and in a proper spirit. A child is harmed if he be unduly checked as a questioner; and he is helped as he could be in no other way, as a truth-seeker, if he be encouraged and wisely trained by his parents in a child's high prerogative as a questioner.

FOURTEEN

TRAINING A CHILD'S FAITH

There is no need of trying to implant faith in a child's nature, for it is there to begin with. But there is need of training a child's faith, so that it shall be rightly directed and wisely developed. Every child has the instinct of faith, as surely as it has the instinct of appetite. The inborn impulse to seek nourishment is not more real and positive in a normal child, than is the impulse in such a child to cling to and to trust another. Both instincts are already there, and both need training.

The faith here spoken of is that faith that rests on a person, not that miscalled "faith" which applies to an assent to a series of dogmas. True faith, indeed, always rests on a person. Any other use of the term is only by accommodation, and is liable to be misleading. One of the best definitions of Christian faith is, "That act by which one person, a sinner, commits himself to another person, a Saviour." Even before a child is old enough to learn of a Saviour, the instinct of faith is one of the child's qualities; just as the instinct of hunger is a child's quality before the child is old enough to know the nature of its fitting food. If a mother, or a nurse, or even a stranger, puts a finger into the chubby hand of an infant, that little hand will close over the proffered finger, and cling to it as for dear life. And it is not until a child has learned to distrust, that it is said to be "old enough to be afraid." While a child's faith is yet undisturbed, as also after a child's faith has become discriminating, a child's faith needs wise directing and developing; and to this end there is need of wisdom and of care on the part of those who have the responsibility of this training.

While the instinct of faith is innate in the child, a knowledge of the One on whom his faith can rest with ultimate confidence is not innate. A knowledge of God comes to man by revelation; and whoever has responsibility for a child's moral training, has the duty of revealing to that child a knowledge of God. But a child can understand God, and can grasp a true conception of Him, quite as easily as the profoundest philosopher can. A child does not need to be led by degrees into a knowledge of God. As soon as he is capable of learning that his voice can be heard by his loving mother or his loving father in another room, he is capable of learning that his voice can be heard by a loving Father whom he has never seen; who is always within hearing, but never within sight; who is the loving Father of his father and mother, as well as of himself and of everybody else; who is able to do all things, and who is sure to do all things well. In the knowledge of this truth, a child can be taught to pray to God in faith, as early as he can speak; and even to know something of the meaning of prayer before he can utter words intelligently.

From the very beginning the child can take in the great truths concerning God's nature, and the scope of God's power, as fully as a theologian can take them in. Therefore there need be no fear that too much is proffered to the child's mind in this sphere, if only it all be proffered in simplicity as explicit truth, without any attempt at its explanation.

Bishop Patteson, in his missionary work among the South Sea Islanders, found it best to begin with John's Gospel, in imparting religious instruction to untutored natives; for they could take that in easier than they could comprehend the historical books of the Bible. It is much the same with children. They can receive the profoundest truths of the Bible without any explanation. When they are older, they will be better fitted to grapple with the difficulties of elementary religious teachings. The idea that a child must have a knowledge of the outline of the Bible story before he knows the central truth that Jesus Christ is his loving Saviour, is as unreasonable as it would be to suppose that a child must know the anatomy of the human frame before he is able to believe in his mother's love for him.

The first lesson in the training of a child's faith is the lesson that he is to have faith in God. Many a child is told to have faith in the power of prayer, or faith in the value of good conduct, without being shown that his faith should rest wholly and absolutely on God. He is told that he can hope to have whatever he prays for; and that if he is a good boy he can expect a blessing, while if he is a bad boy he cannot expect to be blessed. With this training the child's faith is drawn away from God, and is led to rest on his personal conduct; whereas his faith ought to be trained to rest on the God to whom he prays, and in loving obedience to whom he strives to be good.

If you tell a child that God is able and ready to give him everything that he prays for, the child is prompt to accept your statement as a truth, and so he prays for a pleasant day, when a pleasant day is desired by him. If the pleasant day comes accordingly, the child's faith in prayer is confirmed; but if the day be a stormy one, the child's mind is bewildered, and a doubt is likely to creep into his mind whether prayer is always so effective as he had been told to believe it to be. And the case is similar when the child prays for the health of one whom he loves, or for some gift which he longs to receive, or for success in some personal endeavor, and the issue is not in accordance with his petition.

If, however, on the other hand, you plainly tell a child that God knows what is best for us better than we know for ourselves, and that, while God is glad to have us come to Him with all our wishes and all our troubles, we must leave it to God to decide just what He will give to us and do for us, the child is ready to accept this statement as the truth; and then his faith in God is not disturbed in the slightest degree by finding that God has decided to do differently from his request to God in prayer. On every side, children are being taught to have faith in prayer, rather than to have faith in God; and, in consequence, their faith is continually subject to shocks which would never have disturbed it if it had been trained to rest on God instead of resting on prayer.

If you tell a child that God loves good children, and that he does not love bad children, the child will believe you; and then, when he thinks he is a good child, he will be glad that there is a God who can appreciate him; but when he knows he is a bad child, he will perhaps be sorry that there is a God in the universe to be his enemy. So far as your training does its legitimate work, in this instance, the child is trained, not to have faith in God, but to have confidence in his own merits as a means of commending him to the God whom you have misrepresented to him. If, on the other hand, you tell a child that God is love, and that His love goes out unfailingly toward all, even toward those who have no love for Him, and that, while God loves to have children good, He loves them tenderly while they are very bad, the child will take in that great truth gratefully; and then he is readier to have faith in God, and to want to be good because the loving God loves to have him good. And in this way a child's faith in God may be the means of quickening and shaping his desires in the direction of well-doing.

As a means of training a child's faith in God more intelligently and with greater definiteness, the fact of the Incarnation may be disclosed to him in all the fullness of its richest meaning. A very young child can comprehend the truth that God in His love sent His Son into this world as a little child, with the name Jesus—or Saviour; that Jesus grew up from childhood into manhood, that He loved little children, that He died for them, that He rose again from the dead, and ascended into heaven, that still He loves children, that He watches over them tenderly, and that He is ready to help them in all their trials and needs, and to be their Saviour forever. With this knowledge of Jesus as God's representative, a child can be trained to trust Jesus at all times; to feel safe in darkness and in danger because of His nearness, His love, and His power; to be sure of His sympathy, and to rest on Him as a sufficient Saviour. That a child is capable of such faith as this, is not fairly a question. The only question, if question there be, is whether anyone but a child can attain to such faith. One thing is as sure as the words of Jesus are true, and that is, that "whosoever shall not receive the kingdom of God as a little child shall in no wise enter therein"; or, in other words, that a little child's faith is a pattern for the believers of every age.

The training of a child's faith is the most delicate and the most important duty that devolves upon one who is set to the work of child training. More is involved in it for the child's welfare, and more depends upon it for the child's enjoyment and efficiency in life, than pivots on any other phase of the training of a child. He who would train a child's faith aright has need of wisdom, and yet more has need of faith—just such faith as that to the exercise of which he would train the child of his charge. Peculiarly has a parent need to watch lest he check or hinder unduly the loving promptings of a child's faith; for it is our Lord Himself who has said: "Whoso shall cause one of these little ones which believe on me to stumble, it is profitable for him that a great millstone should be hanged about his neck, and that he should be sunk in the depth of the sea."

FIFTEEN

TRAINING CHILDREN TO SABBATH OBSERVANCE

Every day in the week is the Lord's day, for children; but one day in the week is peculiarly the Lord's day, for children as well as for older persons. How to train a child to wise and faithful Sabbath observance, on the Lord's day, is a question that puzzles many a Christian parent; and, as a rule, the more true and loving and Christlike the parent, the greater the practical puzzle at this point. The difficulty in the case is not so much, how to secure the observance of the Sabbath by a child, as it is to decide what should be the proper observance of the Sabbath by a child.

If, indeed, it were simply a question of compelling a child to conform to certain fixed and rigid rules of Sabbath observance, any able-bodied and determined parent, with a stern face, and the help of a birch rod and a dark closet, could compass all the difficulties of the case. But while it is a question of bringing the child to enjoy the loving service of God on God's peculiar day, it requires other qualities than sternness on the parent's part, and other agencies than a birch rod and a dark closet, to meet the requirements of the situation. And so it is that a right apprehension of the nature of a wise and proper observance of the Sabbath is an essential prerequisite of the wise and proper training of children to such an observance.

Love must be at the basis of all acceptable service of God. Any observance of the commands of God which is slavish and reluctant, is sure to lack God's approval. The Sabbath is a sign, or a token, of the loving covenant between God and His people. It is to be borne in mind, it is to be remembered, it is to be counted holy, accordingly. One day in seven is to be given up to loving thoughts of God, to a loving rest from one's own work and pleasure, and to a loving part in the worship of God. On that day, above other days, the thought of God's children should be: "This is the day which the LORD hath made; We will rejoice and be glad in it." How to train children to a joyous observance of the Lord's day, to a joyous looking forward to its coming, and to a joyous looking back upon its memories, is a weightier question, with thoughtful and intelligent Christian parents, than how to conform the conduct of children to the traditional ideas of legitimate Sabbath observance. An utter disregard of the Sabbath in the training of children is a great wrong; but even a greater wrong than this is the training of children to count the Lord's day a day of irksome constraint instead of a delight.

As a child's occupation on other days of the week is different from the occupation of his parents, so a child's occupation on the Lord's day ought to be different from his parent's occupation on that day. It would be cruel, indeed, to insist that on the Lord's day alone a child should be forced to do the same things that his parents do, and that so that day above all others should be a day of toil and of discomfort to a child. For parent and for child alike, the Lord's day should be a day of rest and of worship; but neither for parent nor for child is simple inaction rest; nor is hard Bible study, or merely sitting still in church-time, worship. Rest is to be secured by a change of occupation, and worship is to be performed by turning the thoughts Godward. How to help children to refreshing rest and to joyous worship on the Lord's day, is the practical matter at issue.

To bring a child into habits of loving and reverent Sabbath observance is a matter of training; and that training ought to begin at a very early age of the child, and continue throughout the years of his childhood. Long before a child can know what is the distinctive idea of the Sabbath, or why it is to be observed in a manner peculiar to itself, he can be trained to perceive that one day in seven is different from the other six days, and that its standard is higher and its spirit more joyous; that its tone is quieter, and its atmosphere more reverent. And all this ought to be secured to every child in a Christian home, from the very outset of the child's training to its close. Even a dog, or a horse, or an ox, learns to know and to prize some of the privileges and enjoyments of the Sabbath; and an infant in arms is as capable as one of the brutes of receiving an impression of truth in this realm of fact and sentiment. But in the case of the infant or of the brute everything depends upon those persons who have it in training.

A common cause of trouble in this matter is, that the training does not begin early enough. A child is permitted to go on for months, if not for years, without any direct suggestion of a difference between the Lord's day and other days of the week; and when the first attempt is made to show him that such a difference ought to be recognized, he is already fixed in habits which stand in the way of his recognition, so that the new call on him breaks in unpleasantly upon his course of favorite infantile action. Yet it ought to be so that a child's earliest consciousness of life is linked with the evidences of the greater light and joy and peace of the day that is above other days of the week, in his nursery experiences, and that his earliest habits are in the line of such a distinction as this. And thus it can be.

It is for the parents to make clear the distinction that marks, in the child's mind, the Lord's day as the day of days in the week's history. The child may be differently dressed, or differently washed, or differently handled, on that day from any other. Some more disagreeable detail of his morning toilet, or of his day's management, might on that day be omitted, as a means of marking the day. There may be a sweeter song sung in his hearing, or a brighter exhibit of some kind made in his sight, or a peculiar favor of some sort granted to him, which links a special joy with that day in comparison with the days on either side of it. As soon as the child is old enough to grasp a rattle or to play with a toy, there ought to be a difference between his Sabbath rattle or other toy, and his weekday delights in the same line. By one means or another he should have the Lord's day to look back upon as his brightest memory, and to look forward to as his fondest anticipation. And in this way he can be trained to enjoy the Lord's day, even before he can know why it is made a joy to him. A child is well started in the line of wise training when he is carried along as far as this.

When the anniversary of a child's birthday comes around, a loving parent is likely to emphasize and illustrate to the child the parental love which should make that season a season of gladness and joy to the child. Special gifts or special favors are bestowed on the child at such a time, so that the child shall be sure to welcome each successive return of his birthday anniversary. So, again, when the Christmas anniversary has come, the Christian parent sees to it that the child has a cause of delight in the enjoyments and possessions it brings. It is not that the parents are lacking in love at other times; but it is that the child shall have fresh reminders, at these anniversary seasons, of that love which is unfailing throughout the year. So it ought to be, in the effort to make clear and prominent, on the return of each Lord's day, the love of God which is the same at one time as at another. As the parents will treasure little gifts as loving surprises for their children on the birthday and the Christmas anniversary, so the parents ought to plan to make each new Lord's day a better, brighter day than any other of the week; and to this end the best things for the child's enjoyment may well be kept back until then, as a help to this uplifting of the delights of the day above the weekdays' highest level.

It is customary to keep a child's best clothing for use on the Lord's day. It might well, also, be customary to keep a child's best toys, best pictures, best books, best enjoyments, for a place in the same day of days in the week's round. This is a custom in many a well-ordered Christian home, and the advantages of it are apparent there.

The Sabbath closet, or Sabbath cabinet, or Sabbath drawer, ought to be a treasure house of delights in every Christian home; not to be opened except on the Lord's day, and sure to bring added enjoyment when it is opened in the children's sight. In that treasure house there may be bright colored pictures of Bible scenes; Sunday school papers; books of stories which are suitable and attractive above others for Sabbath reading; dissected maps of Bible lands, or dissected pages of Bible texts, of the Lord's Prayer, or of the Apostles' Creed; models of the Tabernacle, or of Noah's Ark and its inmates. Whatever is there, ought resolutely to be kept there at all other times than on the Lord's day. However much the children may long for the contents of that treasure house, between Sabbaths, they ought to find it impossible to have a view of them until that day of days has come round again. The use of these things should be associated inseparably, in the children's minds, with the Lord's day and its privileges, and so should help to make that day a delight, as a day of God's choicest gifts to those whom God loves and who love Him. By such means the very plays or recreations of the children may be made as truly a means of rest and of worship on the children's part as are the labors of the parents, in the line of Bible study or of Sunday school teaching, a means of Sabbath rest and of Sabbath worship to *them* on each recurring Lord's day.

Even for the youngest children there may be a touch of Sabbath enjoyment in a piece of Sabbath confectionery, or of Sabbath cake, of a sort allowed them at no other time. There are little ones who are not permitted to have candy freely at their own homes, but who are privileged to have a choice bit of this at their grandmother's, where they visit, after Sunday school, on every Lord's day. And there are grown-up children who remember pleasantly that when they were very little ones they were permitted to have a make-believe Sabbath visit together in their happy home, with a table spread with tiny dishes of an attractive appearance, which they never saw except on the Lord's day. There are others who remember with what delight they were accustomed, while children, after a certain age, to sit up and have a place at the family table at tea-time, on Sundays; although on other days they must be in bed before that hour.

If, indeed, the Lord's day is, in any such way, made a day of peculiar delight to children, with the understanding on their part—as they come to years of understanding—that this is because the day is peculiarly the Lord's day, there is a gain to them, so far, in the Lord's plan of the Sabbath for man's welfare in the loving service of the loving God. But if, on the other hand, the first impressions in the children's mind concerning this day of days are, that it is a day of harsh prohibitions and of dreariness and discomfort, there is so far a dishonoring in their minds of the day and of Him whose day it is; and for this result their unwise parents are, of course, responsible.

As children grow older, and are capable of comprehending more fully the spiritual meanings and privileges and possibilities of the Sabbath, they need more help from their parents—not less help, but more—in order to their wise use of the day, and to the gaining of its greatest advantages. The hour of family worship ought to have more in it on the Lord's day than on any other day of the week. Its exercises should be ampler and more varied. Either at that hour, or at some other, the Sunday school lesson for the week should be taken up and studied by parents and children together.

There are homes where the children have a Sunday school of their own, at a convenient hour of the day, in the family room, led by father or mother, or by older brother or sister, with the help of maps and blackboard, or slates. There are other homes in which the father leads a children's service of worship, in the early evening, and reads a little sermon from some one of the many published volumes of sermons for children. Wherever either of these plans is adopted, there should be a part for each of the children, not only in the singing and reading, but in asking and answering questions.

Apart from such formal exercises as these, one child can be showing and explaining a book of Bible pictures or of Scripture cards to younger children; or one group of children can be picking out Bible places or Bible persons from their recent lessons and arranging them alphabetically on slates or on slips of paper, while another group is studying out some of the many Bible puzzles or curious Bible questions which are published so freely for such a purpose. Variety in methods is desirable from week to week, and variety is practicable.

The singing of fitting and attractive songs of joy and praise will naturally have larger prominence, at the hours of family worship, and at other hours of the day and evening, on the Lord's day, than on other days of the week. And parents ought to find time on the Lord's day to read aloud to their children, or to tell them, stories suited to their needs, as well as to lead to familiar conversation with them. For *this* mode of training there can be no satisfactory substitute. Of course, it takes time, and it calls for courage, for high resolve, or self-denial, and for faith. But it is worth more than all it costs.

All this is apart from the question of the attendance and duties of the little ones at the Sunday school or at the place of worship. When a child is of suitable age to have an intelligent part in the exercises of the Sunday school, he should be helped to find those exercises a means of sacred enjoyment. When, at a later day, he is old enough to be at the general service of worship without undue weariness, it is the duty of the parents to make that place a place of gladsomeness to him, as often as he is found there. Not wearisomeness, but rest, is appropriate to the holiest Sabbath services of the Lord's day. Not deepened shadow, but clearer sunlight, is fitting to its sacred hours.

The spirit of the entire day's observances ought to be a reverent spirit; but it should be understood by the parents that true reverence is better shown in gladness than in gloom. Where the Lord's day is counted a dismal one by the children, it is obvious that the parents have failed to train their children to hallow that day, as the day which is peculiarly sacred to the love of their loving Father in heaven. Whether at home, or at Sunday school or any other church service, the children should be helped to realize that the day is a day of brightness and of cheer; that while differing in its occupations and enjoyments from all other days, it is the best of them all. When a little boy, out of a home thus ordered, heard one of his companions express, on Sunday, a wish that it was already Monday, the little fellow said, with evident heartiness, "Why! don't *you* like Sunday? I like it best of all the days." And so it ought to be in the case of every boy and girl in a Christian home.

The difference is not in the children, but in the mode of their training, when in one home the Sabbath is welcomed and in another home it is dreaded by the little ones. Such a difference ought not to exist. By one means or another, or by one means and another, all children ought to be trained to find the Lord's day a day of delight in the Lord's service; and parents ought to see to it that *their* children, if not others, are thus trained. It can be so; it should be so.

TRAINING A CHILD IN AMUSEMENTS

Amusements properly belong to children. A child needs to be amused while he is a child, and because he is a child. It may be a question whether a grown-up person, of average intelligence and of tolerable moral worth, does really need amusements, however much he may need diversion or recreation within due limits; but there can be no fair question as to the need of amusements for a child. And if a child has need of amusements, he has need to be trained in his choice and use of amusements.

How to amuse a child wisely and with effectiveness, is a practical question with a nurse or loving parent, from the time that the little babe first begins to look up with interest at a ball or a trinket swung before his eyes just out of reach of his uplifted hands, or to look and listen as a toy rattle is shaken above him—all the way along until he is old enough to choose his own methods of diversion and recreation. And on the answering of this question much depends for the child's character and happiness; for amusements have their influence in shaping a child's estimates of life and its purposes, and in fitting or unfitting him for the duties he has to perform in life.

There is a wide range of a child's amusements; in their nature, in their tendency, and in the companionships which accompany them. The differences between some of these which may seem but slight at the start, involve differences of principle as well as of method; and they need to be looked at in view of their probable outcome, rather than as they present themselves just now to the surface observer. Indeed, it is the looking for the underlying principle in the attractiveness of a given form of amusement, and for the obvious trend of its influence, that is the primary duty of a parent who would train his children wisely in their amusements, from the earliest beginning of effort to amuse those children.

The center of companionships in a child's amusements ought to be the parents themselves. In the nature of things it is impossible for the parents to be a child's only companions in this line, or to be always his companions; but parents ought, in some way and at some time, to evidence such an interest in their every child's amusements that he will feel that he is as close to his parents, and that his parents are as much to him, in this thing as in any other. If, indeed, a child had no companionship with his parents in his amusements, there would be reared a sad barrier between him and his parents in that sphere of his life which is largest and most attractive while he is at an age to be most impressible.

"One of the first duties of a genuinely Christian parent," says Bushnell, "is to show a generous sympathy with the plays of his children; providing playthings and means of play, inviting suitable companions for them, and requiring them to have it as one of their pleasures, to keep such companions entertained in their plays, instead of playing always for their own mere self-pleasing. Sometimes, too, the parent having a hearty interest in the plays of his children, will drop out for the time the sense of his years, and go into the frolic of their mood with them. They will enjoy no other time so much as that, and it will have the effect to make the authority, so far unbent, just as much stronger and more welcome, as it has brought itself closer to them, and given them a more complete show of sympathy."

A true mother will naturally incline to show a hearty interest in her child's amusements, and she ought to encourage herself to feel that the time taken for this exhibit of her loving sympathy with him is by no means lost time. It may be harder for the father, than for the mother, to give the time or to show the interest essential to this duty; but he ought to secure the benefit of it in some way. A few minutes given to the little ones, as they are privileged to clamber into the father's bed before he is up in the morning, and romp with them there will do much to connect him pleasantly with their playtime. So, again, will a brief season at the close of the day, when he becomes acquainted with their special amusements, and shows that they are much to him, because they are much to his dear ones.

No companionship should be permitted to a child in his amusements that is likely to lower his moral tone, or to vitiate his moral taste. There are cases in which a parent is tempted to allow his children to be taken into a portion of the home establishment, or of the immediate neighborhood, in order that they may be amused by or with the children or the grown persons there, when he would be unwilling to have them under such influences or in such surroundings for any other purpose. This is a great mistake. The companionships of a child in the stable or at the street corner, while he is merely being amused, are likely to be quite as potent and pervasive as those which are around him in the parlor or the dining room, at a time when his nature is not so actively and freely at its fullest play. In fact, the companionships which accompany a child's amusements are an important feature in the training forces of this sphere.

Amusements may be, and ought to be, such as will aid in developing and upbuilding a child's manliness or womanliness. Again, they may be such as will prove an injury to the tastes and character of the child. Even the simplest forms of amusement may have in them the one or the other of these tendencies. A child's earlier playthings and games may have much to do with training his eye and ear and hand and voice and bodily movements. They ought all to be watched and shaped accordingly. This truth is the fundamental one in the kindergarten system; and a study of the methods of that system may be of service to a parent who would learn how to guide a child in his amusements in this direction.

Peculiarly is it important that a child's amusements should not have in them any element of *chance,* as tending to give him the idea that his attainments or progress in life will depend in any measure upon "luck." From his play with building blocks or with jack-straws, up to his games of ball or of chess, every movement that a child is called on to make in the sphere of his amusements ought to be one in which his success or his failure is dependent on his skill or his lack of it. A child may be harmed for life by the conviction that his hope of success in the world rests on that "streak of luck" which seemed to be his in the games of chance he played in boyhood. And a child may be helped for life by the character which was developed in him in his boyhood's games of skill. It was an illustration of this principle, when the Duke of Wellington pointed to the playground of Eton, and said, "It was there that the battle of Waterloo was won."

Children's amusements should be such as do not of themselves involve late hours, or tend directly to the premature developing of their young natures. They should not be such as are likely to become permanent occupations rather than temporary amusements; such as gain a stronger and stronger hold with the passing years instead of being outgrown with childhood; or such as open the way to the child's becoming a professional amusement-maker. They should be such as will have a centripetal rather than a centrifugal force, as related to the home circle.

It ought to be so, in every well-ordered home, that a child can find more pleasure at home than away from home; and this state of things will depend very much upon the kind of amusements that are secured in a child's home. It is not enough that there be amusements at the home, but the amusements there must be those that cannot be engaged in elsewhere as well as there. Many a parent makes the mistake of trying to keep his children at home by introducing amusements there that arouse in the children a desire to go elsewhere for something of the same sort in greater freshness or variety. But wiser parents secure to their children such home amusements as cannot be indulged in to the same advantage outside of that home.

A child may have such a "baby-house," such a collection of dolls and doll furniture, such a "play-closet," such a store of building blocks and mechanical toys, such a cellar or such a garret, in his or her own home, as cannot be found in any other home. To be at home with these will be more attractive than to be in another home without them. There may be such an interest excited in scrapbook making, in picture painting, in candy making, with the advantages for carrying it on, at the child's home, that to go away from home would be a loss, so far, instead of a gain. Singing and music may be such a feature in the home life that the loss of it will be felt outside of that home. So it may be with those social games that involve a measure of intelligence and information not to be found in ordinary homes elsewhere. All such amusements partake of the centripetal rather than the centrifugal force, as related to the children's home; and they have their advantage accordingly. It is for the parents to secure these for the children, or to incur the penalty of their lack.

Children will have amusements, whether their parents choose their amusements for them, or leave the children to choose them for themselves. The amusements of children will tend to the gain or to the loss of the children. It is for parents to decide whether the children shall be left to choose their own amusements, with the probability of their choosing to their own harm; or whether the parents shall choose helpful amusements more attractive than the harmful ones. The result of this choice is an important one to the parents, and a yet more important one to the children.

SEVENTEEN

TRAINING A CHILD
TO COURTESY

U nless a man is courteous toward others, he is at a disadvantage in the world, even though he be the possessor of every other good trait and quality possible to humanity, and of every material, mental, and spiritual acquisition which can belong to mere man. And if a man be marked by exceptional courtesy in all his intercourse with others, he has an advantage to start with in the struggle of life, beyond all that could be his in health and wealth and wisdom without courtesy. Yet courtesy is never wholly a natural quality. It is always a result of training; albeit the training will be far easier in one case than in another.

Courtesy is the external manifestation of a right spirit toward others. Its basis is in an unselfish and a fitting regard for the rights and feelings of those with whom one is brought into intercourse; but the principles of its expression must be a matter of wise study on the part of those who have had experience in the ways of the world, and who would give the benefit of their experience to those who come after them. Courtesy is not merely a surface finish of manners; although courtesy is sure to show itself in a finished surface of manners. Good breeding, politeness, and fine manners, are all included in the term "courtesy"; but these all are the expression of courtesy, rather than its essence and inspiration. "Good breeding," says one, "is made up of a multitude of petty sacrifices." "True politeness," says another, "is the spirit of benevolence showing itself in a refined way. It is the expression of goodwill and kindness." Fine manners, De Quincey says, consist "in two capital features: first of all, respect of others; secondly, in self-respect."

The courteous man is sure not to be lacking in self-respect, but he is sure to be lacking in self-assertion. His self-respect is shown in his sense of a responsibility for the comfort and welfare of others; and his unselfish interest in others causes him to lose all thought of himslf in his effort to discharge his responsibility toward others. His courtesy will be evidenced in what he is ready to do for others, rather than in what he seems to look for from others.

Attractiveness of personal appearance, gracefulness in bearing, tastefulness in dress, elegance in manners, and carefulness in word and tone of voice, may, indeed, all be found where there is no true courtesy. The very purpose on the part of their possessor to be thought courteous, to command respect, and to appear to advantage, may cause him or her to show a lack of courtesy, to fail of commanding respect, and to appear far otherwise than advantageously. On the other hand, there are, for example, ladies whose attractions of face and form are but slight, who care little for dress, who pay no attention to mere manners, who are yet so unselfishly thoughtful of others, in all their intercourse with them, that they are called "just delightful" by everybody who knows them. When they have callers, or when they are making calls, they have absolutely no thought about themselves, their appearance, their modes of expression, or the impression they may make on others. They are for the time being absolutely given up to those with whom they converse. They question and listen with enthusiastic interest; they say kindly words because they feel kindly; they avoid unpleasant subjects of mention, and they introduce topics that cannot but be welcome. Because they keep self out of sight, they win respect, admiration, and affection, beyond all that they would dare hope for. And many a man shows a similar self-forgetfulness in his courteous interest in others, and wins a loving recognition of his courtesy on every side. Real courtesy is, however, impossible, in either sex, except where self is practically lost sight of.

In training a child to courtesy, it is of little use to tell him to be forgetful of himself; but it is of value to tell him to be thoughtful of others. The more a person tries to forget himself, the surer he will be to think of himself. Often, indeed, it is the very effort of a person to forget himself, that makes that person painfully self-conscious, and causes him to seem bashful and embarrassed. But when a child thinks of others, his thoughts go away from himself, and self-forgetfulness is a result, rather than a cause, of his action.

To tell a young person to enter a full room without any show of embarrassment, or thought of himself, is to put a barrier in the way of his being self-possessed through self-forgetfulness. But to send a young person into a full room with a life-and-death message to some one already there, is to cause him to forget himself through filling him with thought of another. And this distinction in methods of training is one to be borne in mind in all endeavors at training children to courtesy.

In order to be courteous, a child must have a care to give due deference to others, in his ordinary salutations and greetings, and in his expression of thanks for every kindness or attention shown to him. So far most parents, who give any thought to a matter like this, are ready to go. But true courtesy includes a great deal more than this; and a child needs training accordingly.

Many a boy who is careful to give a respectful greeting to his superiors on the street, or in the house, and who never fails to proffer thanks for any special favor shown to him, lacks greatly in courtesy in his ordinary intercourse with others, because he has not been trained to feel and to show an unselfish interest in those with whom he is brought face to face. Such a boy is more ready to talk of himself, and of that which has a personal interest to him, than to find out what has an interest to others, and to make himself interested in that, or to express his interest in it if he already feels such an interest. If, indeed, from any reason, he finds himself unable to talk freely of that which immediately concerns him, he is often at a loss for a topic of conversation, and is liable to show awkwardness and embarrassment in consequence. And so while courteous at points of conventional etiquette, a boy of this sort is constantly exhibiting his lack of courtesy.

This liability of a child must be borne in mind by his parents in his training, and it must be guarded against by wise counsel and by watchful inquiry on their part. When a child has a playmate with him in his home, he must be trained to make it his first business to find out what that playmate would enjoy, and to shape his own words and ways in conformity with that standard, for the time being. When a child is going into another home, he must be told in advance of his duty to be a sharer with those whom he meets there, in their employments and pleasures, and to express heartily his sense of enjoyment in that which pleases them. When he returns from a visit from another home, he should be asked to tell what he found of interest there, and what he said about it while there; and he should be commended or counseled in proportion to his well-doing or his lack in his exhibit of courtesy in this connection. When he has been talking with an older person, in his own home or abroad, his parents ought to ascertain just how far he has been lacking in courtesy by putting himself forward unduly, or how far he has shown courtesy by having and evidencing an interest in that which was said to him or done for him by his superior; and kindly comment on his course should be given to him by his parents at such a time.

If, indeed, a child has shown any lack of courtesy toward another, whether a person of his own age or older, he should be instructed to be frank and outspoken in expression of his regret for his course, and of his desire to be forgiven for his fault. True courtesy involves a readiness to apologize for any and every failure, whether intentional or unintentional, to do or say just that which ought to have been done or said; and the habit of frank apologizing is acquired by a child only through his careful training in that direction. He who has any reluctance to proffer apologies on even the slightest cause for them, is sadly lacking in the spirit of courtesy; for just so far as one is thoughtfully considerate of the feelings of another will he want to express his regret that any performance or failure on his part has been a cause of discomfort to another.

All this is, of course, a trying matter to a child, and a taxing matter to a parent; but it is to the obvious advantage of both parties. If a child is seen to be lacking in courtesy, his parents are understood to be at fault in his training, so far. If, on the other hand, a child is not trained to courtesy while a child, he is at a disadvantage from his lack of training, as long as he lives. If he has not been trained to give others the first place in his thoughts while he is with them, and to give open expression to all the interest in them which he really has, he cannot be free and unembarrassed in conversation with any and all whom he meets. If, on the other hand, he has had wise and careful training in this direction, he is sure to be as pleasing as he is courteous to others; and to receive as much enjoyment as he gives, through his courtesy in intercourse with all whom he meets.

Personal embarrassment in the presence of others, and a lack of freedom in the expression of one's interest in others, are generally the result of an undue absorption in one's own interests or appearance, and of one's lack of self-forgetful interest in the words and ways and needs of those whom he is summoned to meet. The surest protection of one's children against these misfortunes, is by the wise training of those children to have an interest in others, and to give expression to that interest, whenever they are with others, at home or abroad; and so to be courteous and to show their courtesy as a result of such training.

EIGHTEEN

CULTIVATING A CHILD'S TASTE IN READING

Reading is to the mind what exercise is to the body," says Addison. "As, by the one, health is preserved, strengthened, and invigorated; by the other, virtue (which is the health of the mind) is kept alive, cherished, and confirmed." And Dr. Johnson adds, "The foundation of knowledge must be laid by reading."

But there is reading, and reading; there is reading that debilitates and debases the mind; as there is reading that strengthens and invigorates it. There is reading that forms the basis of knowledge, and there is reading that lessens the reader's desire for knowledge. A love of reading is an acquired taste, not an instinctive preference. The habit of reading is formed in childhood; and a child's taste in reading is formed in the right direction or in the wrong one while he is under the influence of his parents; and *they* are directly responsible for the shaping and cultivating of that taste.

A child ought to read books that are helpful to his growth in character and in knowledge; and a child ought to love to read these books. A child will love to read such books as his parents train, or permit, him to find pleasure in reading. It is the parent who settles this question—by action or by inaction. It is the child who reaps the consequences of his parents' fidelity or lack in this sphere.

Of course, it is not to be understood that a child is to read, and to love to read, only those books which add to his stock of knowledge, or which immediately tend to the improvement of his morals; for there is as legitimate a place for amusement and for the lighter play of imagination in a child's reading, as there is for recreation and laughter in the sphere of his physical training. As one of the fathers of English poetry has told us, "Books should to one of these four ends conduce, For wisdom, piety, delight, or use"; and that reading which conduces merely to "delight" for the time being, has its essential part in the formation of a character that includes wisdom and piety and useful knowledge. But it is to be understood that no child should be left to read only those books to which his untutored tastes naturally incline him; nor should he be made to read other books simply as a dry task. His taste for instructive books as well as for amusing ones should be so cultivated by the judicious and persistent endeavors of his parents, that he will find enjoyment in the one class as truly as in the other.

"Nonsense songs" and the rhymes of "Mother Goose" are not to be undervalued, in their place, as a means of amusement and of attraction in the direction of a child's earliest reading. Their mission in this realm is as real as that of the toy rattle in the education of a child's ear, or the dancing-jack in the training of his eye. But these helps to amusement are to be looked upon only as aids toward something better; not as in themselves sufficient to an end. So, also, it is with the better class of fairy tales. They meet a want in a child's mind in the developing and exercising of his imagination; and he who has never read them will inevitably lack something of that incitement and enjoyment in the realm of fancy which they supply so liberally. But it is only a beginning of good work in the sphere of a child's reading, when he has found that there is amusement there together with food for his imagination and fancy. And it is for the parent to see that the work thus begun does not stop at its beginning.

There is a place for fiction in the matter of a child's reading. Good impressions can be made on a child's mind, and his feelings can be swayed in the direction of the right, by means of a story that is fictitious without being false. And thus it is that the average Sunday school library book has its mission in the work of child training. But fiction ought not to be the chief factor in any child's reading, nor can influence and impressions take the place of instruction and information in the proper filling of his mind's treasure-chambers. Even if a child were to read only the best religious "storybooks" which the world's literature proffers to him, this reading by itself would not tend to the development of his highest mental faculties, or to the fostering of his truest manhood. Unless he reads also that which adds to his stock of knowledge, and which gives him a fresh interest in the events and personages of the world's history, a child cannot obey the Divine injunction to grow in knowledge as well as in grace, and he will be the loser by his lack.

That a child is inclined by nature to prefer an amusing or an exciting storybook to a book of straightforward fact, everybody knows. But that is no reason why a child should follow his own unguided tastes in the matter of reading, any more than he should be permitted to indulge at all times his preference, in the realm of appetite, for sweet cakes instead of bread and butter, or for candies rather than meat and potatoes. "A child left to himself causeth shame to his mother"—and dishonor to himself, in one sphere of action as in another; and unless a parent cultivates a taste for right reading of every sort on a child's part, that child can never be at his best in the world, nor can his parents have such delight in his attainments as otherwise they might have.

A wise parent can train his children to an interest in any book in which they ought to be interested. He can cultivate in their minds such a taste for books of history, of biography, of travel, of popular science, and of other useful knowledge, that they will find in these books a higher and more satisfying pleasure than is found by their companions in the exciting or delusive narrations of fiction and fancy. Illustrations of this possibility are to be seen on every side. There are boys and girls of ten and twelve years of age whose chief delight in reading is in the realm of instructive fact, and who count it beneath them to take time for the reading of fictitious storybooks—religious or sensational. And if more parents were wise and faithful in this department of child training, there would be more children with this elevated taste in their reading.

It is, however, by no means an easy matter, even though it be a simple one, for a parent to cultivate wisely the taste of his children in their reading. He must, to begin with, recognize the importance and magnitude of his work so far, and must give himself to it from the earlier years of his children until they are well established in the good habits he has aided them to form. He must know what books his children ought to read, and what books ought to be kept away from them. Then he must set himself to make the good books attractive to his children, while he resolutely shuts out from their range of reading those books which are pernicious. All this takes time, and thought, and patience, and determination, and intelligent endeavor on his part; but it is work that is remunerative beyond its extremest cost.

The exclusion of that which is evil is peculiarly important in this realm of effort; for if a child has once gained a love of the exciting incidents of the book of sensational fiction, it is doubly difficult to win him to a love of narrations of sober and instructive fact. Hence every parent should see to it that his child is permitted no indulgence in the reading of high-colored and overwrought works of fiction presented in the guise of truth—with or without a moral; whether they come in books from a neighbor's house, or as a Christmas or birthday gift from a relative, or are brought from the Sunday school library. Fairy tales are well enough in their time and way, if they are read as fairy tales, and are worth the reading—are the best of their kind. Fiction has its place in a child's reading, within due bounds of measure and quality. But neither fancy nor fiction is to be tolerated in a child's reading in such a form as to excite the mind, or to vitiate the taste of the child. And for the limitation of such reading by a child the child's parent must hold himself always responsible. No pains should be spared to guard the child from mental as well as from physical poison.

Keeping bad books away from a child is, however, only one part of the work to be done in the effort at cultivating a child's taste in reading. A child must be led to have an intelligent interest in books that are likely to be helpful to him; and this task calls for skill and tact, as well as patience and persistency on the parent's part. Good books must be looked up by the parent, and when they are put into the child's hand it must be with such words of commendation and explanation as to awaken in the child's mind a desire to become possessed of their contents. The sex and age and characteristics and tendencies of a child, as well as the circumstances and associations of the hour, must all be borne in mind in the choice and presentation of the book or books for a child's reading; and a due regard to these incidents will have its effect on the mind of the child under training.

For example, when the Fourth of July is at hand, or is in some way brought into notice, then is a good time to tell a child briefly about the war of the American Revolution, and to give him a book about the Boys of "Seventy-six." When his attention is called to a picture of the Tower of London, he is in a good mood to read some of the more impressive stories of English history. If he is at the seashore, or among the mountains, on a visit, he can be shown some object of

nature—a shell or a crab, a rock or a tree—as a means of in-
teresting him in a little book about this or that phase of natural history or of woodcraft.

A child's question about Jerusalem, or Athens, or Rome,
may be improved to his advantage by pointing him to the
narrative of the Children's Crusade, or to some of the col-
lections of classic stories in guise for children. An incidental
reference to Africa, or India, or the South Sea Islands, may
open the way for a talk with a child about missions in those
parts of the world, and may be used to give him an interest in
some of the more attractive books in description of missionary
heroes ancient and modern. The everyday mentions of men
and things may, each and all of them, in their order, be turned
to good account, as a help in cultivating a taste in reading, by
a parent who is alert to make use of such opportunities.

A parent ought to be constantly on the watch to suggest
books that are suitable for his child's reading, and to incite
his child to an interest in those books. It is a good plan to
talk with a child in advance about the subject treated in a
book, which the parent is disposed to commend, and to tell
the child that which will tend to awaken his wish to know
more about it, as preparatory to handing the book to him.
Reading with the child, and questioning the child concerning his reading, will intensify the child's interest in his reading, and will promote his enjoyment as he reads.

And so it is that a child's taste in reading will be cultivated steadily and effectively in the right direction by any
parent who is willing to do the work that is needful, and
who is able to do it wisely. A child needs help in this sphere,
and he welcomes help when it is brought to him. If the help
be given him, he will find pleasure as well as profit in its
using; but if he goes on without help, he is liable to go
astray, and to be a lifetime sufferer in consequence.

NINETEEN

THE VALUE OF TABLE TALK

In proportion as man rises in the intellectual scale, does he give prominence to mental and moral enjoyments in conjunction with his daily meals. He who looks upon the table merely as a place for feeding the body, is so far upon the level of the lower order of animals. He who would improve his time there for the advantage of his mind and character, as well as for the supply of his physical wants, recognizes a standard of utility in the humbler offices of daily life that is perceptible only to one whose higher nature is always striving for supremacy above the lower.

With all the tendency to excesses in the line of appetite among the Greeks and Romans in classic times, there were even then gleams of a higher enjoyment at the table through social intercourse than that which mere eating and drinking supplied. When the Perfect Man was here among men, He showed the possibility of making the household meal a means of mental and spiritual improving; and there are no profounder or more precious truths in the record of our Lord's earthly teachings, than those which are found in His words spoken to those who sat with Him eating and drinking at the common meal. The "table talk" of great men has, for centuries, been recognized as having a freeness, a simplicity, and a forcefulness, not to be found in their words spoken elsewhere.

There are obvious reasons why the social talk at daily meals should possess a value not attainable under other circumstances, in the ordinary Christian household. Just there is the place where all the members of the family must be together. However closely and however diversely they may be occupied at other times, when the hour for the household meal has arrived, everything else must be dropped by them all for the one duty of eating and drinking; and they must all come together for that common purpose. In the very nature of things, too, those who have gathered at the family table must, for the time being, have left all their work behind them, and be in a state of relaxation and of kindlier feeling accordingly. Now it is, therefore, that they are freest to speak with one another of matters having a common interest to all, rather than to dwell in absorbed thought on the special duties from which they have, severally, turned away, or toward which they must turn at the meal's close.

It is a matter of fact that those who sit together at a family table, whether as members of the household or as guests there for a season, learn to understand one another, and to give and receive help and inspiration in their social converse, as they could not without the advantage of this distinctive opportunity. It is also a fact that only now and then is there a family circle the members of which recognize at the fullest, and make available at the best, the value of table talk as a training agency for all who have a share in it, or who are under its immediate influence. Yet he who would train his children as they should be trained, cannot ignore this important training agency without serious and permanent loss to them.

With family customs as they are in the United States, there is more of an opportunity here than abroad, for the training of children by means of table talk. In England, and in Europe generally, young children are likely to be by themselves with nurses or governesses, at meal-time, rather than at the table with their parents. But in this country children are, as a rule, brought to the family table at a very early age, and are permitted to be there not merely while the members of the family are there gathered, but on occasions when a guest is, for the time being, made a member of the household circle. Therefore it is that an important feature of child training in American families is the table talk in those families. This feature varies much in different homes; but at its best it is one of the most potent factors in the intellectual and moral training of the young.

Fifty years ago a gentleman of New England had, as a philanthropist, an educator, and an author, an exceptional acquaintance with men of prominence in similar fields of endeavor in this country and abroad. His home was a place of resort for them. He had a large family of children, all of whom were permitted to be at the family table while those guests were present, as well as at other times. The table talk in that home, between the parents and the guests, or between the parents and their children when no guests were present, was in itself "a liberal education." It gave to those children a general knowledge such as they could hardly have obtained otherwise. It was a source of prompting and of inspiration to them in a multitude of directions. Now that they are themselves parents and grandparents, they perceive how greatly they were the gainers by their training through the table talk of their early home; and they are doing what they can to have the value of table talk as a training agency for the young recognized and made effective in the homes which they direct or influence.

In another New England home, the father was a man of quiet thoughtfulness, and at ordinary times a man of peculiar reticence before his children. But at the family table he was accustomed to unbend as nowhere else. He, also, had a large family of children, and there were frequent visitors among them. The utmost freedom of question and of expression was cultivated in the table talk of that home. The spirited discussions carried on there, between father and mother and children and visitors, were instructive, suggestive, and stimulating, in a very high degree. The family table was, in fact, the intellectual and moral center of that home. No other place was so attractive as that. Not a person, young or old, would leave that table until he had to; and now that the survivors of that happy circle are scattered widely, every one of them will say that no training agency did more for him in his early life than the table talk of his childhood's home.

In one home, where parents and children enjoy themselves in familiar and profitable table talk, it is a custom to settle on the spot every question that may be incidentally raised as to the pronunciation or meaning of a word, the date of a personage in ancient or modern history, the location of a geographical site, or anything else of that nature that comes into discussion at the family table. As an aid to knowledge in these lines, there stands in a corner of the diningroom a bookrest, on the top of which lies an English dictionary, while on the shelves below are a biographical dictionary and a pronouncing gazeteer of the world, ready for instant reference in every case of dispute or doubt.

At the breakfast table, in that home, the father runs his eye over the morning paper, and gives to his family the main points of its news which he deems worthy of special note in the family circle. The children there are free to tell of what they have studied in school, or to ask about points that have been raised by their teachers or companions. And in such ways the children are trained to an intelligent interest in a variety and range of subjects that would otherwise be quite beyond their ordinary observation.

One father has been accustomed to treasure up the best things of his experience or studies for each day, with a view to bringing them attractively to the attention of his children at the family table, at the day's close, or at the next day's beginning. Another has had the habit of selecting a special topic for conversation at the dinner table a day in advance, in order that the children may prepare themselves, by thinking or reading, for a share in the conversation. Thus an item in the morning paper may suggest an inquiry about Bismarck, or Gladstone, or Parnell, or Henry M. Stanley; and the father will say, "Now let us have that man before us for our talk tomorrow at dinner. Find out all you can about him, and we will help one another to a fuller knowledge of him." In this way the children are being trained to an ever-broadening interest in men and things in the world's affairs, and to methods of thought and study in their search for knowledge.

There is no end to the modes of conducting table talk as a means of child training; and there is no end to the influence of table talk in this direction, however conducted. Indeed, it may be said with truth, that table talk is quite as likely to be influential as a means of child training when the parents have no thought of using it to this end, as when they seek to use it accordingly. At every family table there is sure to be talking; and the talk that is heard at the family table is sure to have its part in a child's training, whether the parents wish it to be so or not.

There are fathers whose table talk is chiefly in complaint of the family cooking, or in criticism of the mother's method of managing the household. There are mothers who are more given to asking where on earth their children learned to talk and act as they do, than to inquiring in what part of the earth the most important archaeological discoveries are just now in progress. And there are still more fathers and mothers whose table talk is wholly between themselves, except as they turn aside, occasionally, to say sharply to their little ones, "Why don't you keep still, children, while your father and mother are talking?" All this table talk has its influence on the children. It leads them to have less respect for their parents, and less interest in the home table except as a place of satisfying their natural hunger. It is potent, even though it be not profitable.

Table talk ought to be such, in every family, as to make the hour of home mealtime one of the most attractive as well as one of the most beneficial hours of the day to all the children. But in order to make table-talk valuable, parents must have something to talk about at the table, must be willing to talk about it there, and must have the children lovingly in mind as they do their table talking.

TWENTY

GUIDING A CHILD IN COMPANIONSHIPS

A child cannot easily go on through childhood without companions, even if it were desirable for him to do so. Moreover, it is not desirable for a child to go on through childhood without companions, even if it were every way practicable for him to do so. Companions are a necessity to a child, whether the case be looked at in the light of the world as it is, or in the light of the world as it ought to be. Hence, as a child will have companions, and as he needs to have them, it is doubly important that a parent be alive to the importance of guiding his every child in the choice of his companions and in his relations to those companions whom he has without choosing.

No child can be rightly trained all by himself, not yet wholly by means of those agencies and influences that come to him directly from above his head. There are forces which operate for a child's training through being brought to bear upon him laterally rather than perpendicularly; coming in upon him by way of his sympathies, instead of by way of his natural desire for knowledge. There are lessons which a child cannot learn so well from an elder teacher above him as from a young teacher alongside of him. There are impulses which can never be at their fullest with a child when he is alone as a child, but which will fill and sway him when they are operative upon him as one of a little company of children. Only as he learns these lessons from, and receives these impulses with, wisely chosen and fitting companions, can a child have the benefit of them to which he is fairly entitled.

Any observing parent will testify that, on more than one occasion, his child has come to him with a new interest in a thought or a theme, inspired by the words or example of a young companion, to the surprise of the parent—who had before sought in vain to excite an interest in that very direction. All that the parent had said on the subject had been of no value, in comparison with that which had been said or done by the child's companion, as another self. Again, there are few parents who have not found to their regret that their child has received lessons and impulses directly opposed to all the parental counsel and purposes, through a brief and comparatively unnoticed companionship that ought to have been guarded against. And these are but illustrations of the instructive and swaying power of child companionships. Such a power as this ought not to be ignored or slighted by any parent who would do most and best for his child's wise training.

Any thoughtful parent will realize that a child cannot be trained to be unselfishly considerate of his companions; to bear and forbear with companions who are weak or impatient or exacting; to show sympathy with companions who need sympathy, and to minister lovingly to companions who deserve a loving ministry—unless he has companions toward whom he can thus exercise and evidence a right spirit at all times. And no parent will say, or think, that it would be well for a child to be without these elements of character-training in his life-progress.

An only child is naturally at a disadvantage in his home, because he is an only child. He lacks the lessons which playmates there would give him; the impulses and inspirations which he would receive from their fellowship; the demands on his better nature, and the calls on his self-control and self-denial, which would come from their requirements. Parents who have but one child ought to see to it that the lack in this regard is, in a measure, supplied by the companionships of children from other homes. It is, indeed, a mistake for any parent to attempt the training of his child without the help of child companionships. No child can be so inspiringly and symmetrically trained without, as with, these. Even where there are half a dozen or more children in one family, there is still a need of outside companions for each child, of the same age and wants of that child; for it is not possible for any person to bring himself into the same relations with a child as can be entered into by a child of his own years and requirements.

Because a child's companionships are so influential, it is the more important that they be closely watched and carefully guided by the child's parents. In choosing a neighborhood—for a residence or for a summer vacation; in choosing a weekday school; in choosing a Sunday school, where a choice is open to the parents, the companionships thus secured to their child ought to have prominence in the minds of the parents. And when the neighborhood, and week-day school, and Sunday school, are finally fixed upon, the responsibility is still upon the parent to see to it that the best available companionships there are cultivated, and the most undesirable ones are shunned, by the child. Neglect or carelessness at this point may be a means of harm to the child for his lifetime. Attention just here may do more for him than were possible through any other agency.

It is a parent's duty to know who are his child's companions, and to know the character, and course of conduct, and influence upon his child, of every one of those companions separately. Here is where a parent's chief work is called for in

the matter of guiding and controlling his child's companionships. A parent must have his child's sympathy, in order to
gain this knowledge; and a parent must give his sympathy to
his child, in order to be able to use this knowledge wisely. It
may be necessary to keep an open house for these companions, and an open heart and hand to them personally, as it
surely is necessary to keep an open ear to the child's confidences concerning their sayings and doings, if the parent
would know all about them that he needs to know. There
are parents who do all this for and with their children, as an
effective means of guiding those children in their companionships. It is a pity that there are not more who are willing
to do it, in view of all that it may be a means of accomplish-
ing for children.

Knowing his child's companionships, a parent ought to
encourage such of them as are worthiest, and discourage
such as he cannot approve. He ought to help his child to see
the advantages of the one class and the disadvantages of the
other, and to regulate his social intimacies according to the
standards thus set before him. It will not do for a parent to
allow matters in this line to take their own course, and to
accept all companionships for his child just as they may
come to him. He must feel responsible for his child's wise
selection, from among the number of proffered companions,
of those who are to be retained while others are dropped or
avoided. And it devolves upon a parent to see to it that his
child's companionships are of growing value to his companions as well as to himself; that his child's influence over his
very playfellows is for their good, while his good is promoted
by their association with him. A child's companionships,
like those of older persons, ought to be of advantage to both
parties alike, through the very purpose of making them so.

Recognizing the desirableness and importance of companionships for his child, securing the best that are available, learning fully their characteristics and tendencies,

aiding in their sifting, and seeking in their steady uplifting, a parent can do effective service in the way of guiding his child in and through that child's companionships. To neglect this agency of a child's training, would be to endanger his entire career in life, whatever else were done in his behalf.

TWENTY-ONE

NEVER PUNISH A CHILD IN ANGER

Anger is not always wrong. A parent may be angry without sin. And, as a matter of fact, most parents do get angry, whether they ought to or not. Children are sometimes very provoking, and parents are sometimes very much provoked. It is not always wrong to punish a child. A child may need punishing, and it may be a parent's duty to punish a child accordingly. But it is always wrong for a parent to punish a child in anger; and however great may be the need of a child's punishing, a parent ought never to administer punishment to a child while angry.

Here is a rule which, strictly speaking, knows no exception; yet, as a matter of fact, probably nine-tenths of all the punishing of children that is done by parents in this world is done in anger. And this is one of the wrongs suffered by children through the wrongdoing of their parents.

Anger is hot blood. Anger is passion. Anger is for the time being a controlling emotion, fixing the mind's eye on the one point against which it is specifically directed, to the forgetfulness of all else. But punishment is a judicial act, calling for a clear mind, and a cool head, and a fair considering of every side of the case in hand. Anger is inconsistent with the exercise of the judicial faculty; therefore no person is competent to judge fairly while angry.

If, indeed, in any given case, the anger itself be just, the impulse of the angry man may be in the right direction, and the punishment he would inflict a fitting one; but, again, his impulse may be toward a punishment that is not merited. At all events, the man is not in a frame of mind to decide whether or not his impulse is a wise one; and it is his duty to wait until he can dispassionately view the case in another light than that in which it presents itself to his heated brain. No judge is worthy of the office he administers, if he acts on the impulse of his first estimate of a case before him, without taking time to see what can be shown on the other side of that case. And no parent acts worthily who jumps to the punishment of a child while under the impulse of an angry mood.

There are strong provocatives to anger in many a child's conduct, especially to a parent who is of an intense nature, with an inclination to quickness of temper. A child is disobedient at a point where he has been repeatedly told of his duty; he is quarrelsome with his playmates, or insolent toward his nurse; he is persistently irritable, or he gives way to a fit of ungovernable rage; he destroys property recklessly, or he endangers life and limb; he snatches away a plaything from a little brother, or he clutches his hands into his mother's hair; he indulges in foul language, or he utters threats of revenge; he meets a proffered kiss with a slap or a scratch; his conduct may be even that which would excite anger in a saint, but it certainly is such as to excite anger in the average parent — who is not a saint. Then, while the parent is angry, and while punishment seems merited by the child, the temptation of the parent is to administer punishment; but that temptation is one that ought never to be yielded to, or, if yielded to, it is not without sin.

Punishment may be needed in such a case, but the punishment, to be surely just and to be recognized as just, must be well considered, and must be administered in a manner to show that it is not the outcome of passionate impulse. No punishment ought to be administered by a parent at any time that would not be administered by that parent when he was cool and calm and deliberate, and after he had had a full and free talk on the subject with the child, in the child's best state of mind. Whether the punishment that seems to the parent to be the desert of the child, while the parent is still angry, is the punishment that the parent would deem the fitting one in his cooler, calmer moments, can be better decided after the parent has looked at it in both frames of mind, than before he has had the advantage of a view from the standpoint of fuller deliberation.

"What?" inquired a surprised parent, in conversing with the present writer on this very subject, "do you say that I must never punish my boy while I'm angry with him? Why then I should hardly ever punish him at all. It is in the evenings while I am sitting up for him hour after hour, when I've told him over and over again that he must come in early, that I feel like taking hold of him smartly when he does come in. If I should say nothing to him then, but should leave the matter until the next morning, I should sleep off all my feeling on the subject, and he wouldn't be punished at all." And that father, in that statement of the case, spoke for many a parent, in the whole matter of the punishing of a child while angry. The punishment which the child gets is the result of the passion of the parent, not of the parent's sense of justice; and the child knows this to be the case, whether the parent does or not.

How many boxes of the ear, and shakings of the shoulders, and slappings and strikings, and sentences of doom, which the children now get from their parents, would never be given if only the parents refrained from giving these while angry, but waited until they themselves were calm and unruffled, before deciding whether to give them or not! It is

not by any means easy for a parent always to control himself
in his anger, so as to refrain from acting on the impulse
which his anger imparts; but he who has not control of himself is the last person in the world to attempt the control of
others. And not until a parent has himself in perfect control
ought he to take his child in hand for the judicial investigation and treatment of his case as an evildoer.

Of course, there are cases where instant action on the
part of parents in checking or controlling their children's
conduct is a necessity, whether the parent be excited or
calm; but in such cases the action, however vigorous or
severe, is not in the line of punishment, but of conversation.
A child may be thoughtlessly tugging away at the end of a
table-cloth, with the liability of pulling over upon his head
all the table crockery, including the scalding teapot; or he
may be endangering himself by reaching out toward a
lighted lamp, or an open razor. No time is to be lost. If the
child does not respond to a word, he must be dealt with
promptly and decisively. A sharp rap on the fingers may be
the surest available means of saving him from disaster.

So, again, a wayward child may be aiming a missile at a
costly mirror, or at a playmate's head, in a fit of temper. Not
a moment can then be wasted. Angry or not angry, the parent may have to clutch at the child's lifted arm to save property or life. In such a case, wise action is called for, regardless
of the frame of mind of him who acts. But this is the action
of the peacekeeper rather than of the minister of justice.
The parent fills for the moment the place of the policeman
on his beat, rather than of the judge on his bench. The
question of punishment for the child's action is yet to be
considered; and that, again, must be delayed until there is
no anger in the parent's mind.

Anger, in the sense of hot indignation, may, indeed, as
has already been said, be, upon an occasion, a fitting exhibit
of parental feeling; but this is only in those utterly excep-

tional cases in which a child transcends all ordinary limits of misdoing, and is guilty of that which he himself knows to be intolerable. As Dr. Bushnell says at this point, "There are cases, now and then, in the outrageous and shocking misconduct of some boy, where an explosion is wanted; where the father represents God best by some terrible outburst of indignant violated feeling, and becomes an instant avenger, without any counsel or preparation whatever." But this is apart from all questions of punishment as punishment.

A child knows when punishment is administered to him in anger, and when it is administered to him in a purely judicial frame of mind; and a child puts his estimate accordingly on him who administers the punishment. In a city mission-school, many years ago, there was a wild set of boys who seemed to do all in their power to anger and annoy their teachers. Cases of discipline were a necessity there; for again and again a boy attempted violence to a teacher, and force was required to save the teachers from serious harm. But love swayed those teachers even when force on their part was a necessity; and the boys seemed to understand this fully.

There came a time, however, when the young superintendent of that school, who had often held a scholar in check by force, was made public sport of in such way, with the rude linking of a lady teacher's name with his in ridicule, that his self-control failed him for the moment, and he evidently showed this as he took hold of the offender with unwonted warmth. Instantly the boy started back in surprise, with the reproachful exclamation; "Trumbull, you're mad; and that's wicked." Those words taught a lesson to that young superintendent which he has never forgotten. They showed him that his power over those rough boys was a moral power, and that it pivoted on his retaining power over himself. It was theirs to get him angry if they could; but if they succeeded he was a failure, and they knew it. And that lesson is one that parents as well as superintendents could learn to advantage.

When a parent punishes a child only in love, and without being ruffled by anger, the child is readier to perceive the justice of the punishment, and is under no temptation to resent passion with passion. A child who had been told by her father, that if she did a certain thing he must punish her for it, came to him, on his return home, and informed him that she had transgressed in the thing forbidden. He expressed sincere regret for this. "But you said, papa, that you would punish me for it," she added. "Yes, my dear child, and I must keep my word," was his answer. Then, as he drew her lovingly to him, he told her just why he must punish her. Looking up into his face with tearful trust, she said: "You don't like to punish me—do you, papa?" "Indeed I don't, my darling," he said, in earnestness. "It hurts you more than it hurts me—doesn't it, papa?" was her sympathetic question, as if she were more troubled for her father than for herself. "Yes, indeed it does, my darling child," was his loving rejoinder. And the punishment which that father gave and that daughter received under circumstances like these, was a cause of no chafing between the two even for the moment, while it brought its gain to both, as no act of punishment in anger, however just in itself, could ever bring, in such a case.

As a rule, a child ought not to be punished except for an offense that, at the time of its committal, was known by the child to be an offense deserving of punishment. It is no more fair for a parent to impose a penalty to an offense after the offense is committed, than it is for a civil government to pass an *ex post facto* law, by which punishment is to be awarded for offenses committed before that law was passed. And if a child understands, when he does a wrong, that he must expect a fixed punishment as its penalty, there is little danger of his feeling that his parent is unjust in administering that punishment; and, certainly, there is no need of the parent hastening to administer that punishment while still angry.

Punishment received by a child from an angry parent is an injury to both parent and child. The parent is the worse for yielding to the temptation to give way to anger against a child. The child is harmed by knowing that his parent has done wrong. A child can be taught to know that he deserves punishment. A child needs no teaching to know that his parent is wrong in punishing him while angry. No parent ought to punish a child except with a view to the child's good. And in order to do good to a child through his punishing, a parent must religiously refrain from punishing him while angry.

TWENTY-TWO

SCOLDING IS NEVER IN ORDER

Many a father who will not strike his child feels free to scold him. And a scolding mother is not always deemed the severest and most unjust of mothers. Yet, while it is sometimes right to strike a child, it is at no time right to scold one. Scolding is, in fact, never in order, in dealing with a child, or in any other duty in life.

To "scold" is to assail or revile with boisterous speech. The word itself seems to have a primary meaning akin to that of barking or howling. From its earliest use the term "scolding" has borne a bad reputation. In common law, "a common scold" is a public nuisance, against which the civil authority may be invoked by the disturbed neighborhood. This is a fact at the present time, as it was a fact in the days of old. And it is true today as it was when spoken by John Skelton, four centuries ago, that "A sclaunderous tunge, a tunge of a skolde, Worketh more mischiefe than can be tolde."

Scolding is always an expression of a bad spirit and of a loss of temper. This is as truly the case when a lovely mother scolds her child for breaking his playthings wilfully, or for soiling his third dress in one forenoon by playing in the gutter which he was forbidden to approach, as when one apple-woman yells out her abuse of another apple-woman in a street-corner quarrel. In either case the essence of the scolding is in the multiplication of hot words in expression of strong feelings that, while eminently natural, ought to be held in better control. The words themselves may be very different in the two cases, but the spirit and method are much alike in both. It is scolding in the one case as in the other; and scolding is never in order.

If a child has done wrong, a child needs talking to; but no parent ought to talk to a child while that parent is unable to talk in a natural tone of voice, and with carefully measured words. If the parent is tempted to speak rapidly, or to multiply words without stopping to weigh them, or to show an excited state of feeling, the parent's first duty is to gain entire self-control. Until that control is secured, there is no use of the parent's trying to attempt any measure of child training. The loss of self-control is for the time being an utter loss of power for the control of others. This is as true in one sphere as in another.

Mr. Hammond's admirable work on dog-training, already referred to in these pages, says on this very point, to the dog-trainer: "You must keep perfectly cool, and must suffer no sign to escape of any anger or impatience; for if you cannot control your temper, you are not the one to train a dog." "Do not allow yourself," says the instructor, "under any circumstances to speak to your pupil in anything but your ordinary tone of voice." And, recognizing the difficulties of the case, he adds: "Exercise an unwearied patience; and if at any time you find the strain upon your nerves growing a little tense, leave him at once, and wait until you are perfectly calm before resuming the lesson." That is good counsel for him who would train a dog—or a child; for in either dog-training or child training, scolding—loud and excited talking—is never in order.

In giving commands, or in giving censure, to a child, the fewer and the more calmly spoken words the better. A child soon learns that scolding means less than quiet talking; and he even comes to find a certain satisfaction in waiting silently until the scolder has blown off the surplus feeling which vents itself in this way. There are times, indeed, when words may be multiplied to advantage in explaining to a child the nature and consequences of his offense, and the reasons why he should do differently in the future; but such words should always be spoken in gentleness, and in self-controlled earnestness. Scolding—rapidly spoken censure and protest, in the exhibit of strong feeling—is never in order as a means of training and directing a child.

Most parents, even the gentler and kindlier parents, scold their children more or less. Rarely can a child say, "My parents never scold me." Many a child is well trained in spite of his being scolded. Many a parent is a good parent not-withstanding the fact that he scolds his children. But no child is ever helped or benefited by any scolding that he receives; and no parent ever helps or benefits his child by means of scolding. Scolding is not always ruinous, but it is always out of place.

If, indeed, scolding has any good effect at all, that effect is on the scolder, and not on the scolded. Scolding is the outburst of strong feeling that struggles for the mastery under the pressure of some outside provocation. It never benefits the one against whom it is directed, nor yet those who are its outside observers, however it may give physical relief to the one who indulges in it. If, therefore, scolding is an unavoidable necessity on the part of any parent, let that parent at once shut himself, or herself, up, all alone, in a room where the scolding can be indulged in without harming any one. But let it be remembered that, as an element in child training, scolding is never, never in order.

TWENTY-THREE

DEALING TENDERLY
WITH A CHILD'S FEARS

The best child in the world is liable to be full of fears; and the child who is full of fears deserves careful handling, in order that his fears may not gain permanent control of him. Fears are of a child's very nature, and every child's training must be in view of the fact that he has fears. How to deal wisely, firmly, and tenderly with a child's fears is, therefore, one of the important practical questions in the training of a child.

To begin with, it should be understood that a child's fears are no sign of a child's weakness, but that, as a rule, the stronger a child is in the elements of a well-balanced and an admirable character, the more fears he will have to contend with in the exercise of his character. Hence a child's fears are worthy of respect, and call for tenderness of treatment, instead of being looked at as a cause of ridicule or of severity on the part of those who observe them.

"Fear" is not "cowardice." Fear is a keen perception of dangers, real or imaginary. Cowardice is a refusal to brave the dangers which the fears recognize. Fear is the evidence of manly sensitiveness. Cowardice is the exhibit of unmanly weakness. Fear is a moral attribute of humanity. Cowardice is a moral lack. A child, or a man, who is wholly free from cowardice, may have more fears than the veriest coward living. The one struggles successfully against his many fears; the other yields in craven submission to the first fear that besets him.

It is by no means to a child's credit that it can be said of him, "He doesn't know what fear is." A child ought to know what fear is. He is pitiably ignorant if he does not. The same is true of the bravest man. It is not the soldier who does not know fear but it is the soldier who will not yield to the fears he feels, who is the truly courageous man. Without a fine perception and a quick apprehension of dangers on every side, no soldier could be fully alive to the necessities of his position and to the demands of his duty; and it is, in a sense, peculiarly true, that the best soldier is likely to be the most fearful. It is the Braddocks who are "not afraid" that needlessly suffer disaster; while the Washingtons who have timely fears are prepared to act efficiently in the time of disaster. There is a suggestion of this truth in the words of the Apostle, "Let him that thinketh he standeth take heed lest he fall"; or, as it might be said, "Let him who has no fears have a care lest he fail from his lack of fears."

A child's fears are on various planes, and because of this they must be differently dealt with. A child has fears which are reasonable, fears which are unreasoning, and fears which are wholly imaginary; fears which are the result of a process of reasoning, fears which are apart from any reasoning process, and fears which are in the realm of fancy and imagination. In one child one phase of these fears is the more prominent, and in another child another phase. But in every child there is a measure of fear on all three of these planes.

A child who has once fallen trying to stand or walk, or from coming too near the top of a flight of stairs, is liable to be afraid that he will fall again if he makes another effort in the same direction. "A burnt child dreads fire." That is a reasonable fear. Again, a child comes very early to an instinctive shrinking from trusting himself to a stranger; he recoils from an ill-appearing person or thing; he trembles at a loud noise; he is fearful because of the slamming of shutters, even when he knows that the wind does it; he is afraid of thunder as well as of lightning, apart from any question of harm to him from the electric bolt. This is without any process of reasoning on his part, even while there is a basis of reality in the causes of his fear. Yet again, a child is afraid of being alone in the darkness; or he is afraid of "ghosts" and "goblins," about which he has been told by others. It is his imagination that is at work in this case.

That all these different fears should call for precisely the same treatment is, of course, an absurdity. How to deal with each class of fears by itself, is an important element in the question before the parent who would treat wisely the fears of his children.

A child would be obviously lacking in sense, if he were never afraid of the consequences of any action to which he was inclined. If he had no fear of falling, no fear of fire or water, no fear of edged tools or machinery, no fear of a moving vehicle, it would be an indication of his defectiveness in reasoning faculties. Yet that there is a wide difference among children in the measure of their timidity in the presence of personal danger, no one will deny.

One child inclines to be unduly cautious, while another inclines to be unduly venturesome. Moreover, that the timidest child can be brought to overcome, in large measure, his fears of physical harm, is apparent in view of the success of primitive peoples in training their children to swim before they can walk, or to climb as soon as they can stand; and of circus managers in bringing the children of civilized parents to feats of daring agility. How to train a child to the mastery of his fears in this line, without the brutal disregard of his feelings that too often accompanies such training by savages or professional athletes, is a point worthy of the attention of every wise parent.

Because these fears are within the realm of the reasoning faculties, they ought to be removed by means of a process of reasoning. A child ought not to be beaten or threatened or ridiculed into the overcoming of his fears, but rather encouraged and directed to their overcoming, through showing him that they ought to, and that they can, be overcome. His fears are not unworthy of him; therefore he ought neither to be punished nor to be made sport of because he has them. The meeting and surmounting of his fears, within bounds, is also worthy of a child; therefore he ought to be helped to see this fact, and kindly cheered and sympathized with in his efforts accordingly.

Many a child has been trained to intelligent fearlessness, so far as he ought to be fearless, through the wise and tender endeavors of his parents to show him his power in this direction, and to stimulate him to the exercise of this power. And many a child has been turned aside from the overcoming of his fears, through the untimely ridicule of him for his possession of those fears. Because he must be a laughing-stock while struggling to master his fears, he decides to evade the struggle in order to evade the ridicule. Tenderness in pointing out to a child the wiser way of meeting his fears, is better than severity on the one hand, or ridicule on the other.

Unreasoning or instinctive fears are common to both the brightest and the dullest children. They are among the guards which are granted to humanity, in its very nature, for its own protection. It would never do for a child to make no distinction between persons whom he could trust implicitly, and persons whom he must suspect, or shrink from. It is right that he should be won or repelled by differences in form and expression. He needs to be capable of starting at a sudden sound, and of standing in awe of the great forces of nature. The proper meeting of these instinctive fears by a child must be through his understanding of their reasonable limits, and through the intelligent conforming of his action to that understanding. It is for the parent to train his child to know how far he must overcome these fears, and how far they must still have play in his mind. And this is a process requiring tenderness, patience, and wisdom.

When a child shows fear at the moaning of the wind about the house, and at its rattling of the shutters on a winter's night, it is not fair to say to him, "Oh, nonsense! What are you afraid of? That's nothing but the wind." There is no help to the child in that saying; but there is harm to him in its suggestion of the parent's lack of sympathy with him. If, however, the parent says, at such a time, "Does that sound trouble you? Let me tell you how it comes"; and then goes on to show how the wind is doing God's work in driving away causes of sickness, and how it sometimes makes sweet music on wires that are stretched out for it to play upon—the child may come to have a new thought about the wind, and to listen for its changing sounds on the shutters or through the trees.

One good mother sought to overcome her little boy's fear of thunder by simply telling him that it was God's voice speaking out of the heavens; but that was one step too many for his thoughts to take as yet. The thunder just as it was, was what gave him trouble, no matter where it came from; so when the next peal sounded through the air, the little fellow whimpered out despairingly, "Mamma, baby doesn't like God's voice." And that mother was too wise and tender to rebuke her child for his unreadiness for that mode of revelation from above.

On the other hand, an equally wise and tender father, whose little daughter was afraid of the thunder, took his child into his arms, when a thunderstorm was raging, and carried her out on to the piazza, in order, as he said, to show her something very beautiful. Then he told her that the clouds were making loud music, and that the light always flashed from the clouds before the music sounded, and he wanted her to watch for both light and music. His evident enthusiasm on the subject, and his manifest tenderness toward his child, swept the little one away from her fears, out toward the wonders of nature above her; and soon she was ready to believe that the thunder was as the very voice of God, which she could listen to with reverent gratitude. If there were more of such loving wisdom exercised in parental dealing with children's fears, there would be less trouble from the unmastered fears of children on every side.

The hardest fears to control are, however, the fears which are purely of the imagination; and no other fears call for such considerate tenderness of treatment as these, in the realm of child training. It is the more sensitive children, children of the finest grain, and of the more active and potent imaginings, who are most liable to the sway of these fears, and who are sure to suffer most from them. Persons who are lacking in the imaginative faculty, or who are cold-blooded and matter-of-fact in their temperament and nature, are hardly able to comprehend the power of these fears over those who feel them at their fullest. Hence it is that these fears in a child's mind are less likely than any others to receive due consideration from parents generally, even while they need it most.

Because these fears are not of the reason, they are not to be removed by reason. Because they are of the imagination, the imagination must be called into service for their mastery. It is not enough to pronounce these fears unreasonable and foolish. They are, in their realm, a reality, and they must be met accordingly. While children suffer from them most keenly, they are not always outgrown in manhood. A clergyman already past the middle of life was heard to say that, to this day, he could never come up the cellar stairs all by himself, late at night, after covering up the furnace fire for the night, without the irrational fear that some one would clutch him by his feet from out of the darkness below. The fear was a reality, even though the cause was in the imagination. And a soldier who had been under fire in a score of battles, said that he would today rather go into another battle than to be all alone in a deserted house in broad daylight.

In neither of these cases was the person under the influence of superstitious fears, but only of those fears which an active imagination will suggest in connection with possibilities of danger beyond all that can yet be seen. And these are but illustrations of the sway of such fears in the minds of men who are stronger by reason of their very susceptibility to such fears. These men have added power because of their vivid imaginations; and because of their vivid imaginations they are liable to fears of this sort. What folly, then, to blame a child of high imagination for feeling the sway of similar fears!

The heroic treatment of these fears of the imagination is not what is called for in every instance; nor is it always sufficient to meet the case. A child may be trained to go by himself into the darkness, or to sleep in a room shut away from other occupants of the house, without overcoming his fears of imagination. And if these fears be constantly spoken of as those which are utterly unworthy of him, the child may indeed refrain from giving expression to them, and suffer all by himself with an uncalled-for sense of humiliation, even while he is just as timid as before. It would be better, in many a case, to refrain from an undue strain on a sensitive child, through sending him out of the house in the evening to talk a lonely path, or through forcing him to sleep beyond the easy call of other members of the household; but in every instance it is right and wise for a parent to give his child the evidence of sympathy with him in his fears, and of tender considerateness of him in his struggles for their overcoming.

The help of helps to a child in meeting his fears of the imagination, is found in the bringing to his mind, through the imagination, a sense of the constant presence of a Divine Protector to cheer him when his fears are at their highest. A little child who wakened in the middle of the night, called to her parents, in another room, and when her father was by her bedside, she told him that she was afraid to be alone. Instead of rebuking her for this, he said, "There's a little verse in the Bible, my darling, that's meant for you at a time like this; and I want you to have that in your mind whenever you waken in this way. It is a verse out of one of David's psalms; and it is what he said to the Lord his Shepherd; 'What time I am afraid, I will trust in thee.' That is the verse. Now, whenever you are afraid, you can think of that verse, and say it over as a loving prayer, and the Good Shepherd will hear you, and will keep you from all harm."

The child repeated the verse after her father, and she saw its peculiar fitness to her case. As her father then prayed to the God of David in loving confidence, she realized more fully than before how near God was to her in the time of her greatest fears. And from that time on, that little child was comforted through faith when her imagination pressed her with its terrors. She never forgot that verse; and it still is a help to her in her fears by day and by night.

A child's imagination ought, indeed, to be guarded sacredly. It should be shielded as far as possible from unnecessary fears, through foolish stories of ghosts and witches, told by nurses or companions, or read from improper books. But whether a child's fears in this realm be few or many, they should be dealt with tenderly by a loving parent; not ignored, nor rudely overborne. Many a child has been harmed for life through a thoughless disregard by his parents of the fears of his imagination. But every child might be helped for life by a sympathetic and tender treatment of these fears, on the part of his parents, while he is still under training.

In no realm of a child's nature has a child greater need of sympathy and tenderness from his parents, than in the realm of his fears. It is because he is sensitive, and in proportion as he is sensitive, that a child's fears have any hold upon him. And a child's sensitiveness is too sacred to be treated rudely or with lightness by those to whom he is dearest, and who would fain train him wisely and well.

TWENTY-FOUR

THE SORROWS
OF CHILDREN

The trials and sorrows of children and young people have not always had the recognition they deserve from parents and teachers. It is even customary to speak of childhood as an age of utter freedom from anxiety and grief, and to look upon boys and girls generally as happier and lighterhearted then they can hope to be in later life. No mistake could be greater than this. The darker side of life is seen first. The brighter side comes afterward.

"Man is born unto trouble, as the sparks fly upward." The first sound of a child's voice is a cry, and that cry is many times repeated before the child gives his first smile. How easily the best-behaved baby cries, every mother can testify. It is the soothing of a crying child, not the sharing in the joy of a laughing one, which taxes the skill and the patience of a faithful nurse. Only as the child is trained, disciplined, to overcome his inclination to cry, and to find happiness in his sphere, does he come to be a joyous and glad-hearted little one.

Every burden of life—and life's burdens seem many—rests at its heaviest on a child's nature. A child is refused more requests than are granted to him. He is subjected to disappointments daily, almost hourly. The baby cannot reach the moon, nor handle papa's razor, nor pound the looking glass, nor pull over the teapot, nor creep into the fire. The older child cannot eat everything he wants to, nor go out at all times, nor have papa and mamma ever at his side. Then there come school-tasks to shrink from, and the jealousies and unkindnesses of playmates and companions to grieve over. And as more is known of life and the world, and the inevitable struggles with temptation, and of the injustice and wrongs which must in so many instances be suffered, it becomes harder and harder for a young person to see only the brighter side of human existence, and to bear up bravely and cheerily under all that tends to sadden and oppress us. There are more clouds in the sky of life's April than of life's August.

As the young grow older they come to be less sensitive to little trials, and they control themselves better. They are not tempted to shed tears whenever they find their plans thwarted, or themselves unable to do or to have all they would like to, or their companions unlike what they had hoped for. They learn to philosophize over their troubles, to look at the compensations of life, and to recognize the fact that many things which they have longed after would not have been good for them if they had obtained them, and that, at all events, time will soften many of their trials. And so life's troubles seem lighter, and life's joys greater—if not more intense—to maturer minds than to the young. Even when men are far greater sufferers than ever children can be, they come to be calloused in a measure through the very continuance of their grief, and they bear as a little thing that which would have crushed them a few years before.

But how their former experiences and their earlier tumults of feeling are forgotten by men and women as they get farther and farther away from childhood! They fail to re-member how deeply they grieved as little ones. They forget, in large measure, how heavy the burdens of life seemed in their earlier years. They are sure that many things which now trouble them had no power over them when they were younger. It seems to them, indeed, that the little trials of children cannot seem very large even to children. And so, as they watch the little ones in their brighter moments, they think that childhood is the age of freedom from sorrow and care; and they are even inclined to wish that they were young once more, they they might have no such hours of trial and grief as now they are called to so frequently.

Values are relative; so are losses; so are sorrows. One person puts a high estimate on what another deems quite worthless. One grieves over a loss for which another would feel no concern. That which a child values highly may be of no moment to the child's father; but its loss might be as great a grief to the child as would the loss to the father of that which, in the father's sight, is incalculably more important. The breaking of a valued toy may be as serious a disaster, from the child's point of view, as the bankrupting of the father's business would seem from the father's standpoint. And the child's temporary censure by his playmates for some slight misdoing of his, may cause to him as bitter a sorrow as would the condemnation by the public, cause to his father when the father's course had brought him into permanent disgrace.

A little girl was startled by what she heard said at the family table concerning a neighbor's loss of household silver through a visit of robbers. "Mamma," she whispered, "do robbers take *dolls?*" Her dolls were that child's treasure. If *they* were in danger, life had new terrors for her. "No, my dear," said her mamma; "robbers don't want dolls. Why should they take them?" "I didn't know but they would want them for their little girls," was the answer; as showing that, in the child's estimation, dolls had a value for children in the homes of robbers as well as elsewhere. With the assurance that her dolls were safe, that little girl had less fear of midnight robberies. What, to her mind, was the loss of the family silver, or of clothing and jewels, if the dolls were to be left unharmed! A child's estimate of values may be a false one; but the child's sorrows over losses measured by those estimates are as real as any one's sorrows.

It must, indeed, be a sore pressure of sorrow and trial on a child's mind and heart, to bring him to commit suicide; yet the suicide of a child is by no means so rare an act as many would suppose. The annual official statistics of suicides in France show a considerable percentage of children among the unhappy victims. Hundreds of suicides are reported in England, year by year. In America the case is much the same. Month by month the public prints give the details of child suicides as a result of some sore trial or sorrow to the little ones.

"Forgive me for committing suicide," wrote a bright and affectionate lad, in a note to his father just before committing the fatal act. "I am tired of life," he added. And everything in connection with his suicide showed that that lad had planned the act with a cool head and an aching heart. In fact, most persons of adult years can recall out of the memories of their earlier life some experiences of disappointment, or of grief, or of a sense of injustice, which made life seem to them for the time being no longer worth living, and the thought of an end to their trial in death not wholly terrible. Very *childish* all this was, of course; but that is the point of its lesson to parents; childish griefs are very real and very trying—to children.

One plain teaching of these facts concerning the sorrows of children is, that the young need the comfort and joys of a Christian faith for the life that now is, quite as surely as the aged need a Christian hope for the life that is to come. The surest way of bringing even a child to see the brighter side of this life is by inducing him to put his trust in an omnipotent

Saviour, who loves him, and who makes all things work together for good to him if only he trust himself to His care and walks faithfully in His service. The invitations and the promises of the Bible are just what children need, to give them happiness and hope for now and for hereafter.

TWENTY-FIVE

THE PLACE OF SYMPATHY IN CHILD TRAINING

A child needs sympathy hardly less than he needs love; yet ten children are loved by their parents where one child has his parents' sympathy. Every parent will admit that love for his children is a duty; but only now and then is there a parent who realizes that he ought to have sympathy with his children. In fact, it may safely be said that, among those children who are not called to suffer from actual unkindness on the part of their parents, there is no greater cause of unhappiness than the lack of parental sympathy. And, on the other hand, it is unquestionably true that in no way can any parent gain such power over his child for the shaping of the child's character and habits of life as by having and showing sympathy with that child.

Love may be all on one side. It may be given without being returned or appreciated. It may fail in influencing or affecting the one toward whom it goes out. But sympathy is in its very nature a twofold force. It cannot be all on one side. From its start it is a response to another's feelings or needs. It is based on the affections, or inclinations, or sufferings, or sense of lack, already experienced by another. Hence sympathy is sure of a grateful recognition by the one who has called it out. Love may be proffered before it is asked for or desired. Sympathy is in itself the answer to a call for that which it represents. Love may, indeed, be unwelcome. Sympathy is, in advance, assured of a welcome.

In his joys as in his sorrows a true child wants someone to share his feelings rather than to guide them. If he has fallen and hurt himself, a child is more helped by being spoken to in evident sympathy than by being told that he must not cry, or that his hurt is a very trifling matter. The love that shows itself in tenderly binding up his wound, in a case like this, has less hold upon the child than the sympathy that expresses a full sense of his pain, and that recognizes and commends his struggle to control his feelings under his injury. It is easier, indeed, to comfort a child at such a time, and to give him power over himself, by showing him that you feel with him, and how you want him to feel, than by telling him, never so lovingly, what he ought to do, and how to do it. And it is the same with a child in any time of joy, as in every time of grief. He wants your sympathy with him in his delights, rather than your loving approval of his enjoying himself just then and in that way.

Herbert Spencer, who makes as little of the finer sentiments of human nature as any intelligent observer of children can safely do, emphasizes this desire of a child for sympathy, in the realm of mental development. "What can be more manifest," he asks, "than the desire of children for intellectual sympathy? Mark how the infant sitting on your knee thrusts into your face the toy it holds, that you too may look at it. See, when it makes a creak with its wet finger on the table, how it turns and looks at you; does it again, and again looks at you; thus saying as clearly as it can—'Hear this new sound.' Watch how the older children come into the room exclaiming, 'Mamma, see what a curious thing,' 'Mamma, look at this,' 'Mamma, look at that;' and would continue the habit, did not the silly mamma tell them not to tease her. Observe how, when out with the nursemaid, each little one runs up to her with the new flower it has gathered, to show her how pretty it is, and to get her also to say it is pretty. Listen to the eager volubility with which every urchin describes any novelty he has been to see, if only he can find some one who will attend with any interest."

How many parents there are, however, who are readier to provide playthings for their children than to share the delights of their children with those playthings; readier to set their children at knowledge-seeking, than to have a part in their children's surprises and enjoyments of knowledge-attaining; readier to make good, as far as they can, all losses to their children, than to grieve with their children over those losses. And what a loss of power to those parents as parents, is this lack of sympathy with their children as children. There are, however, parents who sympathize with their children in all things; and as a result, they practically train and sway their children as they will: for when there is entire sympathy between two persons, the stronger one is necessarily the controlling force with both.

In order to sympathize with another, you must be able to put yourself in his place, mentally and emotionally; to occupy, for the time being, his point of view, and to see that which he sees, and as he sees it, as he looks out thence. It is not that your way of looking at it is his way from the start, but it is that his way of looking at it must be your way while you are taking your start in an effort to show your sympathy with him. In many relations of life, sympathy would be impossible between parties, because of the differences of taste and temperament and habits of thought; but in the case of parent and child, the parent ought to be able to learn the child's ways of thinking and modes of feeling, so as to come into the possibility of sympathy with the child at all times.

How the child ought to feel is one thing. How the child does feel is quite another thing. The parent may know the former better than the child does; but the latter the child knows better than the parent. Until a parent has learned just how the child looks at any matter, the parent is incapable of so coming alongside of the child in his estimate of that matter as to win his confidence and to work with him toward a more correct view of it. To stand off apart from the child, and tell him how he ought to think and feel, may be a means of disheartening him, as he finds himself so far from the correct standard. But to stand with the child and point him to the course he ought to pursue, is more likely to inspire him to honest efforts in that direction, until he comes to think and to feel as his parents would have him.

A parent misses an opportunity of gaining added power over his child, when he fails to show sympathy with that child in the child's enjoyments and ordinary occupations. If, indeed, the parent would be always ready to evidence an interest in his child's plays and companionships and studies, the parent would grow into the very life of his child in all these spheres; and there would be hardly less delight to the child in talking those things over with his parent afterward, than in going through with them originally. But if the parent seems to have no share with the child in any one or all of these lines of childhood experience, the child is necessarily shut away so far from his parent, and compelled to live his life there as if he were parentless.

Still more does a parent lose of opportunity for good to his child, if he fails to have sympathy with his child in that child's weaknesses and follies and misdoings. It is in every child's nature to long for sympathy at the point where he needs it most; and when he has done wrong, or has indulged evil thoughts, or is feeling the force of temptation, he is glad to turn to some one stronger and better than himself, and make confession of his faults and failures. If, as he comes to his parents at such a time, he is met with manifest sympathy, he is drawn to his parents with new confidence and new trust. But if he is met unsympathetically, and is simply told how wrong he is, or how strange it seems that he should be so far astray, he is turned back upon himself to meet his bitterest life-struggle all by himself; and a new barrier is reared between him and his parents, that no parental love can remove, and that no parental watchfulness or care can make a blessing to either child or parent.

It is a great thing for a parent to have such sympathy with his child that his child can tell him freely of his worst thoughts or his greatest failures without any fear of seeming to shock that parent, and so to chill the child's confidence. It is a great thing for a parent to have such sympathetic thoughts of his child when that child has unintentionally broken some fragile keepsake peculiarly dear to the parent, as to be more moved by regret for the child's sorrow over the mishap than for the loss of the precious relic. There is no such power over children as comes from such sympathy with children.

There is truth in the suggestion of Herbert Spencer, that too often "mothers and fathers are mostly considered by their offspring as friend-enemies"; and that it is much better for parents to *show* to their children that they are "their best friends," than to content themselves with *saying so*. It ought to be so, that children would feel that they could find no such appreciative sympathy from any other person, in their enjoyments or in their sorrows and trials, as they are sure of from their parents. This is so in some cases; and wherever it is so, the parents have such power over and with their children as would otherwise be impossible. On the other hand, there are parents who love their children without stint, and who would die to promote their welfare, who actually have no sympathy with their children, and who, because of this lack of sympathy, are without the freest confidences of their children, and are unable to sway them as they fain would.

The power of sympathy is not wholly a natural one. It is largely dependent upon cultivation. An unsympathetic parent may persistently train himself to a habit of sympathy with an unsympathetic child, by recognizing his duty of learning how the child thinks and feels, and by perceiving the gain of getting alongside of that child in loving tenderness in order to bring him to a better way of thinking and feeling. But if a parent and child are not in sympathy, the best and most unselfish love that that parent can give to that child will be fruitless for such results in child training as would be possible if that love were directed by sympathy.

TWENTY-SIX

INFLUENCE OF THE HOME ATMOSPHERE

In the world of nature, life is dependent on the atmosphere. Whatever else is secured, the atmosphere is essential to life's existence. It is, in fact, the atmosphere that gives the possibility of all the varied forms of vegetable and animal life in the earth and the sea and the air. So, again, the atmosphere brings death to every living thing, if elements that are hostile to life prevail in its composition. When the question of the date of man's first appearance on our planet is under discussion, a chief factor in the unsolved problem is the nature of the atmosphere of the earth at any given period of antiquity. Without a life-sustaining atmosphere, life was an impossibility. Similarly, the question of the probability of other planets being inhabited, pivots on this consideration. Life and death are in the atmosphere.

It is not alone the component elements of the atmosphere that bring life or death to all within its scope; but the temperature and the measure of movement of the atmosphere go far to decide the degree of life that shall be attained or preserved within the scope of its influence. Unless there is a due measure of oxygen in the air, the atmosphere is death-giving. Without sufficient warmth to the air, its oxygen is of no avail for the sustaining of life. And even though the oxygen and the warmth be present, the force of the swift-moving air may carry death on its vigorous wings. No gardener would depreciate the importance of a right atmosphere for his most highly prized plants; nor would any wise physician undervalue the sanitary importance of the atmospheric surroundings of his patients. As it is in the natural world, so it is in the moral sphere: life and death are in the atmosphere.

A vital question in connection with every home is, "Is the atmosphere of this home suited to the life and growth, to the developing of the vigor and beauty, of a child's best nature?" That question cannot always be answered in the affirmative; and where it cannot be, it is of little use to talk of the minor training agencies which are operative in behalf of the children in that home.

The atmosphere of a home is the spirit of that home, as evidenced in the conduct and bearing of the parents, and of all whom the parents influence. The atmosphere itself—there, as in all the natural world—is not seen, but is felt. Its effects are clearly observable; but as a cause it is inferred rather than disclosed. Indeed, the better the atmosphere in a home, the more quietly pervasive its influence. Only as the home atmosphere is inimical to the best interests of those who feel its power, does that atmosphere make itself manifest as an atmosphere, rather than give proof of its existence in results that cannot otherwise be accounted for.

You enter one home, and, mingling with the family there, you feel the balmy air of love and sympathy. Parents and children seem to live for one another, and to be in complete accord in all their enjoyments and occupations; and all is restful in the peace that abides there. You are sure that everything in the moral and social atmosphere of that home tends to the fostering and growth of whatever is best in the child-nature. It is obvious that it is easier for a child to be good, and to do well, in such a home as that, than in many another home.

You enter another home, and the chill of the household air strikes you unpleasantly, at the first greeting given to you by any member of the family. There is a side of the child-nature that you know needs more warmth than that for its developing. Again it is the burning heat of an excited and ever-driving household life that you are confident is withering the more delicate and sensitive tendrils of the young hearts being trained there. Yet again, it is the explosive storm-bursts of passion which tear through the air, that make a home a place of peril to the young for the time being, however it may seem in the lulls between tempests. In the one case as in the others, it is the home atmosphere that settles the question of the final tendency of the home training.

In view of the importance of the home atmosphere, parents ought to recognize their responsibility for the atmosphere of the home they make and control. It is not enough for parents to have a lofty ideal for their children, and to instruct and train those children in the direction of that ideal. They must see to it that the atmosphere of their home is such as to foster and develop in their children those traits of character which their loftiest ideal embodies. That atmosphere must be full of pure oxygen of love to God and love to man. It must be neither too hot in its intensity of social activities, nor too cold in its expressions of family affection, but balmy and refreshing in its uniform temperature of household living and being. It must be gentle and peaceful in its manner and movement of sympathetic intercourse. All this it may be. All this is ought to be.

Every home has its atmosphere, good or bad, health-promoting or disease-breeding. And parents are, in every case, directly responsible for the nature of the atmosphere in their home; whether they have acted in recognition of this fact, or have gone on without a thought of it. In order to secure a right home atmosphere for their children, parents must themselves be right. They must guard against poisoning the air of the home with unloving words or thoughts; against chilling it with unsympathetic manners, or overheating it with exciting ways; against disturbing its peaceful flow with restlessness, with fault-findings, or with bursts of temper.

Parents must, as it were, keep their eyes on the barometer and the thermometer of the social life of the home, and see to it that its temperature is safely moderated, and that it is guarded against the effect of sudden storms. Only as such care is taken by wise parents, can the atmosphere in their home be what the needs of their children require it to be.

TWENTY SEVEN

THE POWER OF A MOTHER'S LOVE

In estimating the agencies which combine for child-shaping through child training, the power of a mother's love cannot be overestimated. There is no human love like a mother's love. There is no human tenderness like a mother's tenderness. And there is no such time for a mother's impressive display of her love and tenderness toward her child as in the child's earliest years of his life. That time neglected, and no future can make good the loss to either mother or child. That time improved, and all the years that follow it shall give added proof of its improvement.

Even when a man seems to be dead to every other influence for good, the recollection of a mother's prayers and a mother's tears often has a hold upon him which he neither can nor would break away from. And a mother is so much to a man when he is a man, just because she was all in all to him when he was a child.

Although God calls Himself our Father, He compares His love with the love of a mother, when He would disclose to us the depth of its tenderness, and its matchless fidelity. "As one whom his mother comforteth, so will I comfort you," He says, as if in invitation to the sinner to come like a grieved and tired child, and lay down his weary head on his mother's shoulder, where he is sure of rest and sympathy, and of words of comfort and cheer. "Can a woman forget her nursing child, that she should not have compassion on the son of her womb?" asks God, as if to turn attention to that which is truest and firmest of anything we can know of human affection and fidelity. And then to show that He is a yet surer support than even mothers prove to their loved children, He adds, "Yea, they may forget, yet will not I forget thee."

David, the man after God's own heart, could find no words which could express his abiding confidence in God, like those wherein he declares, "When my father and my mother forsake me, then the LORD will take me up." Nor could he find any figure of the profoundest depth of human sorrow more forcible than that in which he says of himself, "I bowed down heavily, as one that mourneth for his mother." When David's greater Son was hanging on the cross in agony, with the weight of a lost world upon Him, He could forget all His personal suffering, and could turn, as it were, for a moment, from the work of eternal redemption, to recognize the tenderness and fidelity of His agonized mother at His feet, and to commend her with His dying breath to the faithful ministry of the disciple whom He loved.

The Bible abounds with pictures of loving mothers and of a mother's love—Hagar, weeping in the desert over her famishing boy; Rachel mourning for her children, refusing to be comforted because they were not; Jochebed playing the servant to secure the privilege of nursing her babe for the daughter of Pharoah; Hannah joying before God over her treaure of a longed-for son; the true mother in the presence of Solomon, ready to lose her child that it might be saved; Rizpah, watching on the hilltop the hanging bodies of her murdered sons, month after month, from the beginning of harvest until the autumn rains, suffering "neither the birds of the air to rest on them by day, nor the beasts of the field by night"; the wife of Jeroboam, longing to be at the bedside of her dying son, and torn at heart with the thought that as soon as she should reach him there he must die; the widow of Zarephath, and the Shunammite woman, securing the intercession of the prophet for the restoration to life of their dead darlings; the mother of James and John pleading with Jesus for favors to her sons; the Syro-Phoenician woman venturing everything, and refusing to be put aside, that she might win a blessing from Him who alone was able to restore to health and freedom her grievously vexed daughter; the mother of Timothy, teaching her son lessons by which the world is still profiting; and so on through a long list of those who were representative mothers, chosen of God for a place in the sacred record, and whose like are about us still on every side.

And the Bible injunctions concerning mothers are as positive as the examples of their loving ministry are numerous. "Honor thy father and thy mother" is a commandment which has preeminence in the reward attached to it. "Forsake not the law of thy mother," said Solomon; "and despise not thy mother when she is old." It is indeed a "foolish man," as well as an unnatural one, who "despiseth his mother," or who fails to give her gratitude and love so long as she is spared to him. In all ages and everywhere, the true children of a true mother "rise up and call her blessed"; for they realize, sooner or later, that God gives no richer blessing to man than is found in a mother's love. Even in the days when a queen-wife was a slave, a queen mother was looked up to with reverence, not because she had been a queen, but because she was still the king's mother. "A mother dead!" wrote gruff and tenderhearted Carlyle. "It is an epoch for us all; and to each one of us it comes with a pungency as if peculiar, a look as of originality and singularity." And it was of the mother whose death called out this ejaculation, of whom, while she was still living, Carlyle had written, "I thought, if I had all the mothers I ever saw to choose from, I would have chosen my own."

A mother can never be replaced. She will be missed and mourned when she has passed away, however she may be undervalued by the "foolish son" to whom she still gives the wealth of her unappreciated affection. Indeed, the true man never, while his mother is alive, outgrows a certain sense of dependence on a loving mother's sympathy and care. His hair may be whitened with age; he may have children, and even grandchildren, looking up to him in respect and affection; but while his mother lives she is his mother, and he is her boy. And when she dies he for the first time realizes the desolateness of a motherless son. There is then no one on earth to whom he can look up with the never-doubting confidence and the never-lacking restfulness of a tired child to a loving mother. There is a shelter taken away from above his head, and he seems to stand unprotected, as never before, from the smiting sun and the driving storms of life's pilgrimage. He can no more be called "My dear son" in those tones which no music of earth can equal. To him always: "A mother is a mother still, The holiest thing alive."

Biography is rich with illustrations of this truth, although the man whose mother is still spared to him need not go beyond his own experience to recognize its force. Here, for example, is testy old Dr. Johnson, bearish and boorish in many things. When he is fifty years old, and his mother is ninety, he writes to her in tenderness: "You have been the best mother, and, I believe, the best woman, in the world. I thank you for your indulgence to me, and beg forgiveness of all that I have done ill, and of all that I have omitted to do well." How many men there are whom the world little thinks of as childlike, who could make these words their own, and set their hands to them with Johnson's closing assurance, "I am, dear, dear mother, your dutiful son." And the lionhearted Luther, who seems better suited to thunder defiance at spiritual oppressors than to speak words of trustful affection to a kindhearted woman, turns from his religious warfare to write to his aged and dying mother: "I am deeply sorrowful that I cannot be with you in the flesh, as I fain would be." "All your children pray for you."

St. Augustine has been called the most important convert to the truth from St. Paul to Luther. Near the close of his eventful life, St. Augustine said: "It is to my mother that I owe everything. If I am thy child, O my God! it is because thou gavest me such a mother. If I prefer the truth to all things, it is the fruit of my mother's teachings. If I did not long ago perish in sin and misery, it is because of the long and faithful years which she pleaded for me." And of his mother's remembered devotedness to him, he said at the time of her death: "O my God! what comparison is there between the honor that I paid to her, and her slavery for me?"

John Quincy Adams's mother lived to be seventy-four; but he had not outgrown his sense of personal dependence upon her, when she was taken away. "My mother was an angel upon earth," he wrote. "She was the real personification of female virtue, of piety, of charity, of ever-active and never-intermitting benevolence. O God! could she have been spared yet a little longer!" "I have enjoyed but for short seasons, and at long, distant intervals, the happiness of her society, yet she has been to me more than a mother. She has been a spirit from above watching over me for good, and contributing, by my mere consciousness of her existence, to the comfort of my life. That consciousness has gone, and without her the world feels to me like a solitude." When President Nott, of Union College, was more than ninety years old, and had been for half a century a college president, as strength and sense failed him in his dying hours, the memory of his mother's love was fresh and

potent, and he could be hushed to needed sleep by patting
him gently on the shoulder, and singing to him the familiar
lullabies of long ago, after the fashion of that mother, who
he fancied was still at hand to care for him.

Lord Macaulay has been called a cold-hearted man, but
he was never unmindful of the unique preciousness of a
mother's love. He it was who said: "In after life you may
have friends, fond, dear, kind friends, but never will you
have again the inexpressible love and gentleness lavished
upon you which a mother bestows. Often do I sigh, in my
struggles with the hard, uncaring world, for the sweet deep
security I felt when, of an evening, nestling in her bosom, I
listened to some quiet tale, suitable to my age, read in her
untiring voice. Never can I forget her sweet glances cast
upon me when I appeared asleep; never, her kiss of peace at
night. Years have passed since we laid her beside my father
in the old churchyard, yet still her voice whispers from the
grave and her eye watches over me as I visit spots long since
hallowed to the memory of my mother."

Napoleon Bonaparte, with all his self-reliance and personal independence of character, never ceased to look up to
his mother with a reverent affection, and he was accustomed to say that he owed all that he was, and all that he
had, to her character and loving ministry. "Ah, what a
woman! where shall we look for her equal?" he said of her.
"She watched over us with a solicitude unexampled. Every
low sentiment, every ungenerous affection, was discouraged
and discarded. She suffered nothing but that which was
grand and elevated to take root in our youthful understand-
ings. . . . Losses, privations, fatigue, had no effect on her.
She endured all, braved all. She had the energy of a man
combined with the gentleness and delicacy of a woman."

When all else seemed lost to him, as he lay a lonely
prisoner on the shores of St. Helena, Napoleon was sure of
one thing. "My mother loves me," he said; and the thought

of his mother's love was a comfort to him then. He who had felt able to rule a world unaided, was not above a sense of grateful dependence on a love like that. "My opinion is," he said, "that the future good or bad conduct of a child depends entirely upon its mother."

A young army officer lay dying, at the close of our American civil war. He had been much away from home even before the war; and now for four years he had been a soldier in active army service. On many a field of battle he had faced death fearlessly, and in many an hour of privation and hardship he had been dependent on his own strength and resources. What could more have tended to wean a man from reliance on a mother's presence and sustaining care? The soldier's mind was wandering now. It was in the early morning, after a wakeful, restless night. Exciting scenes were evidently before his mind's eye. The enemy was pressing him sorely. He was anxious as to his position. He gave orders rapidly and with vehemence. His subordinates seemed to be failing him. Everything was apparently wrong. Just then the young officer's mother, who had come from the North to watch over him, entered the room where he lay. As the door opened for her coming, he turned toward it his troubled face, as if expecting a new enemy to confront him. Instantly, as he saw who was there, his countenance changed, the look of anxiety passed away, the eye softened, the struggle of doubt and fear was at an end, and with a deep-drawn sigh of relief he said in a tone of restful confidence, "Ah, mother's come! It's all right now!" And the troubled veteran soldier was a soothed child again.

Soldier, statesman, scholar, divine; every man is a child to his mother, to the last; and it is the best that is in a man that keeps him always in this childlikeness toward his loving mother. Were it not for the power of a mother's love, that best and truest side of a man's nature would never be developed, for the man's good and for the mother's reward. It costs something to be a good mother; but there is no reward which earth can give to be compared with that love which a faithful mother wins and holds from the son of her love. Oh! if good mothers could only know how much they are doing for their children by their patient, long-suffering, gentle ways with them, and how sure these children are to see and feel this by and by, the saddest of them would be less sad and more hopeful, while toiling and enduring so faithfully, with perhaps apparently so slight a return.

TWENTY-EIGHT

ALLOWING PLAY TO A CHILD'S IMAGINATION

Imagination is a larger factor in the thoughts and feelings of a child than in the thoughts and feelings of an adult; and this truth needs to be recognized in all wise efforts at a child's training. The mind of a child is full of images which the child knows to be unreal, but which are nonetheless vivid and impressive for being unreal. It is often right, therefore, to allow play to a child's imagination, when it would not be right to permit the child to say, or to say to the child, that which is false.

A child who is hardly old enough to speak perceives the difference between fact and fancy, and is able to see that the unreal is not always the false. Hence a very young child can understand that to "make believe" to him is not to attempt to deceive him. A child in his mother's lap, who is not yet old enough to stand alone, is ready to pull at a string fastened to a chair in front of his mother's seat, and play that he is driving a horse. As he grows older, he will straddle a stick and call that riding horseback; telling his parent, perhaps, of the good long ride he is taking. Not only is it not a parent's duty to tell that child that the chair or the stick is not a horse, but it would be unfair, as well as unkind, to insist on that child's admission that his possession of a horse is only in his fancy.

The child is here not deceived to begin with; therefore, of course, he does not need to be undeceived. Yet it would be wrong for the parent to permit his child to say, as if in reality, that he had been taken out to ride by his father, when nothing of the kind had happened. In the latter case the statement would be a false one, while in the former case it would be only a stretch of fancy. The child as well as the parent would have no difficulty in recognizing the difference between the two statements.

A little girl will delight herself with setting a table with buttons for plates and cups, from which she will serve bread and cake and tea to her invited guests; and she will be lovingly grateful for her mother's apparently hearty suggestion that "this tea is of a fine flavor," when she would feel hurt if her mother were to tell her, coolly and cruelly, that it was only a dry button which had been passed as a cup of tea. The fancy in this case is truer by far than the fact. There is no deception in it; but there is in it the power of an ideal reality. And it is by the dolls and other playthings of childhood that some of the truest instincts of manhood and of womanhood are developed and cultivated in the progress of all right child training.

It is in view of this distinction that the story of Santa Claus and Christmas Eve may be made one of reprehensible falsity, or one of allowable fancy. The underlying idea of Santa Claus is, that on the birth-night of the Holy Child Jesus there comes a messenger from Him to bring good gifts to children. So far the idea is truth. Just how the messenger from Jesus comes, and just who he is, are matters in the realm of fancy. The child is entitled to know the truth, and is entitled also to indulge in a measure of fancy. For a parent to take a child, the night before, and show him all the Christmas gifts arranged in a drawer as preparatory to the stocking-filling, leaving no room for the sweet indulgings of fancy, would neither be wise nor be kind. It would not accord with the God-given needs of the child's nature. Nor, again, would it be wise or kind for the parent to tell the full story of Santa Claus and his reindeers as if it were an absolute literal fact. Children have, indeed, been frightened by the belief that Santa Claus would come down the chimney at night, and would refuse them presents if they were awake at his coming; and this is all wrong. The child should be taught the truth as the truth, and indulged in the fancy as fancy.

It is, indeed, much the same in this realm as in the Bible realm. To say that Jesus is the Good Shepherd is to present a truth in the guise of fancy; and unless a child is helped to know the measure of truth and to perceive the sweep of fancy, there is a danger of trouble in using this Bible figure; for it is a fact that children have suffered from the thought that they were to be literal "lambs" in the Saviour's fold. This recognition of the limits between the fanciful and the false needs to be borne in mind at every stage of a child's training. The false is not to be tolerated. The fanciful is to be allowed in large place.

This truth applies also to the realm of fairy tale reading. A child can read choice fairy tales, understanding that they are fanciful, with less danger to his mind and character than he would incur in the reading of a falsely colored religious storybook. In the one case he knows that the narration is wholly fanciful, while in the other case he is liable to be misled through the belief that what is both fictitious and false may have been a reality. Not the wholly fanciful, but the fictitiously false, in a child's reading, is most likely to be a means of permanent harm to him.

A child's imagination can safely be allowed large play, in his amusements, in his speech, and in his reading. He knows the difference between the fanciful and the false quite as well as his parents do. It is the line between the false and the real in moral fiction that he needs help in defining. It will be well for him if he has parents who understand that distinction, and who are ready to give him help accordingly.

TWENTY-NINE

GIVING ADDED VALUE TO A CHILD'S CHRISTMAS

Christmas is a day of days to the little folks, because of the gifts it brings to them. But Christmas gifts have a greater or a lesser value in the eyes of children according to the measure of the giver's self which is given with them. It is not that children intelligently prize their gifts, as older persons are likely to, in proportion as they read in them the proofs of the giver's loving labor in their preparation. But it is that to children the Christmas gifts by themselves are of minor value, in comparison with the interest excited in the manner of their giving, through labors that really represent the giver's self, whether the children perceive this, at the time, or not.

The Christmas stocking and the Christmas tree give added value to the gifts that they cover; and neither tree nor stocking can be made ready for Christmas morning without patient and loving labor, on the part of the parents, during the night before. Moreover, beyond the dazzling attractions of the ornamented tree, and the suggestive outline of the bulging stocking, the more there is to provoke curiosity and to incite endeavor, on the children's part, in the finding and securing of their Christmas portion, the better the children like it, and the more they value that which is thus made theirs.

It takes time and work and skill to make the most, for the children, of a Christmas morning; but it pays to do this for the darlings, while they still are children. They will never forget it; and it will be a precious memory to them all their life through. It is one of the child training agencies which a parent ought to be glad to use for good.

One good man might be named who has brought to per-fection the art of making Christmas delightful to children. He has no children of his own; so he makes it his mission to give happiness to other people's children. The story of bright and varied Christmas methods in his home would fill a little volume. His plans for Christmas are never twice alike; hence the children whom he gathers say truly, "There was never anything like *this* before." Take a single Christmas for example. This child-lover was busy getting ready for it for weeks in advance. Money he spent freely, but he did not stop with that. Day and evening, with a loving sister's help, he worked away getting everything just to his mind—which was sure to be just to the children's mind. At last Christmas Eve was here; so were the children—nieces and nephews, and others more remote of kin, gathered in his home to wait for the hoped-for day.

Christmas morning came at last. Waking and sleeping dreams had all been full of coming delights to the children; for they knew enough from the past to be sure that good was in store for them. No one overslept, that morning. According to orders, they gathered in the breakfast-room. Their stockings were hanging from the mantel, but limp and empty. Not one suspicious package or box was to be seen. Breakfast was first out of the way, that the morning might be free for a right good time. Then the day was fairly open. Each went to his or her stocking. There was nothing in it but a little card, pendent from a thread coming over the mantel edge. On that card was a rhyming call to follow the thread wherever it might lead; somewhat after this form:

> Charley, dear, if you'll follow your nose,
>   And your nose will follow this string
> Throughout the house, wherever it goes, —
>   You will come to a pretty thing.

Every stocking told the same story, in varied form, and every child stood holding a frail thread, wondering to what it would lead, and waiting the signal for a start. At the word, all were off together.

It was a rare old house, richly furnished with treasures of art and fancy from all the world over. The breakfast room was heavily paneled in carved wood and hung with ancient Gobelin tapestry. The threads which the children followed passed back of the large Swiss clock, along the wall under the tapestry, out by the parlor with its Cordova-leather panels, into a picture-hung reception room, and there mounted to the ceiling above, up through the colored glass skylight. When the children saw that, they scampered through the marble-tiled hall, up the broad polished walnut staircase to the passage above, and there drew up their threads, and started on a new hunt.

From this fresh point of departure the different threads took separate directions. They led hither and thither, the children following, almost holding their breaths with the excitement of pursuit and expectation. Along the corridor walls, under rows of Saracen tiles and Italian majolica and Sèvres porcelain, back of old paintings, through the well-filled library, into and out of closets stored with fishing tackle and hunting gear, through rooms spread with Turkish mats and rich with coverings of Persian embroidery, up into the third story, and down along the underside of the banister rail, back to the lower floor, again the threads led the

way and the children followed. It was a happy hour for old
and young.

By and by the threads came once more to a common
point, passing under a closed door out of a rear hall, where a
printed placard called on each child to wait until all were
together. One by one they came up with beaming faces and
bounding hearts. The door was opened. There in the center
of the disclosed room were seven mammoth pasteboard
Christmas boots, holding from one to three pecks each,
marked with the names of the several children, and filled to
overflowing. Each child seized a boot, and hurried, as
directed, back to the breakfast room.

Then came new surprises. All hands sat on the floor together. Only one package at a time was opened, that all might
enjoy the disclosures to the full. And there were unlooked-
for directions on many a package. One child would take a
package from her Christmas boot, and, on removing the
first wrapper, would find a written announcement that the
package was to be handed over to her cousin. A little later,
the cousin would be directed to pass along another package
to a third one of the party. And so the morning went by.
How happy those children were! What lifelong memories of
enjoyment were then made for them! And how thoroughly
the good uncle and aunt enjoyed that morning with its happiness which they had created!

There were elegant and fitting presents found in those
Christmas boots; but the charm of that day was in the mys-
teries of that pursuing chase all over that beautiful house,
and in the excitements of prolonged anticipation and wonder. Those children will never have done enjoying that
morning. The choicest gifts then received by them had an
added value because their generous giver had put so much
of himself into their preparation and distribution. And this
is but an illustration of a truth that is applicable in the
whole realm of efforts at gladdening the hearts of the little

ones on Christmas or any other day. It matters not, so far, whether the home be one of abundance or or close limitations, whether the gifts be many or few, costly or inexpensive.

He who would make children happy must do for them and do with them, rather than merely give to them. He must give himself with his gifts, and thus imitate and illustrate, in a degree, the love of Him who gave Himself to us, who is touched with the sense of our enjoyments as well as our needs, and who, with all that He gives us, holds out an expectation of some better thing in store for us: of that which passeth knowledge and understanding, but which shall fully satisfy our hopes and longings when at last we have it in possession.

GOOD-NIGHT WORDS

If there is one time more than another when children ought to hear only loving words from their parents, and be helped to feel that theirs is a home of love and gladness, it is when they are going to bed at night. Good-night words to a child ought to be the best of words, as they are words of greatest potency. Yet not every parent realizes this important truth, nor does every child have the benefit of it.

The last waking thoughts of a child have a peculiar power over his mind and heart, and are influential in fixing his impressions and in shaping his character for all time. When he turns from play and playmates, and leaves the busy occupations of his little world, to lie down by himself to sleep, a child has a sense of loneliness and dependence which he does not feel at another time. Then he craves sympathy; he appreciates kindness; he is grieved by harshness or cold neglect.

How glad a true child is to kneel by his mother's knee to pray his evening prayer, or to have his father kneel with him as he prays! How he enjoys words of approval or encouragement when they precede the good-night kiss from either parent! With what warm and grateful affection his young heart glows as he feels the tender impress of his mother's hand or lips upon his forehead before he drops asleep. How bright and dear to him that home seems at such an hour! How sorry he is for every word or act of unkindness which he then recalls from his conduct of the day! How ready he then is to confess his specific acts of misdoing, and all his remembered failures, and to make new resolves and purposes of better doing for the future!

Whatever else a child is impatient to grow away from, he does not readily outgrow the enjoyment of his mother's good-night. As long as she is willing to visit his bedside, and give him a kiss, with a loving word, just before he goes to sleep, he is sure to count that privilege of his home as something above price, and without which he would have a sense of sad lack. And at no time is he more sure than then to be ready to do whatever his mother would ask of him; at no time do gentle, tender words of loving counsel from her sink deeper into his heart, or make an impression more abiding and influential.

There are young men and women, still at their childhood's home, who look for their mother's coming to give them her good-night kiss, with no less of interest and grateful affection than when they were little boys and girls. And there are many more people—both young and old—away from their homes, who thank God with all their hearts for the ineffaceable memories of such tokens of their dear mother's love, while yet they were with her.

Notwithstanding this, however, there is perhaps no one thing in which parents generally are more liable to err than in impatient or unloving words to their children when the little ones are going to bed. The parents are tired, and their stock of patience is at the lowest. If the children are not as quiet and orderly and prompt as they should be, the parents rebuke them more sharply than they would for similar offenses earlier in the day. Too often children go to bed smarting under a sense of injustice from their parents, and brood over their troubles as they try to quiet themselves down to sleep. Their pillows are often wet with their tears of sorrow, and their little hearts are, perhaps, embittered and calloused through the abiding impressions of the wrong they have suffered, or the harshness they have experienced, while they were most susceptible to parental influences for good or ill.

It is a simple matter of fact that some parents actually postpone the punishment of their children for the misdeeds of the day until the leisure hour of twilight and bedtime. A great many mothers besides the "old woman who lived in a shoe," in providing for a large family of children, have often "whipped them all soundly, and sent them to bed." Perhaps children, as a rule, receive more whippings at bedtime than at any other of the twenty-four hours. And unquestionably they then have more scoldings.

"Do you hear me, children?" sounds out the voice of many a mother into the nursery as the children are getting to bed. "If you don't stop playing and talking, and go right to sleep, I'll come up there and just *make* you." And that is the echo of that mother's voice which rings longest in her children's ears.

Again, there are mothers who, without any thought of unkindness, are unwise enough to deliberately refuse a good-night kiss to their children, as a penalty for some slight misconduct; not realizing the essential cruelty of withholding from the little ones this assurance of affection, at a time when the tender heart prizes it above all else. The first effect of such a course as this is to cause bitterness of grief to the children. The repetition of such a course is liable to loosen the parent's loving hold on the little ones, and to diminish the value of the good-night kiss. It is, indeed, probably true, that more children out of reputable homes are soured, and estranged, and are turned astray, through harshness and injustice, or by unwise severity, at their bedtime hour, than from any other provoking cause in their home-life.

Even where there is no harshness of manner or severity of treatment on the part of the parents, there is often an unwise giving of prominence, just then, to a child's faults and failures, so as to sadden and depress the child unduly, and to cast a shade over that hour which ought to be the most hopeful and restful of all the waking hours. Whatever is said by a parent in the line of instruction toward a better course, at such a time, should be in the way of holding up a standard to be reached out after, rather than of rebuking the child's misdoings and shortcomings in the irrevocable past. The latest waking impressions of every day, on every child, ought to be impressions of peace and joy and holy hope.

A sensitive, timid little boy, long years ago, was accustomed to lie down to sleep in a low "trundle-bed," which was rolled under his parents' bed by day, and was brought out for his use by night. As he lay there by himself in the darkness, he could hear the voices of his parents, in their lighted sitting room, across the hallway, on the other side of the house. It seemed to him that his parents never slept; for he left them awake when he was put to bed at night, and he found them awake when he left his bed in the morning. So far this thought was a cause of cheer to him, as his mind was busy with imaginings in the weird darkness of his lonely room.

After loving good-night words and kisses had been given him by both his parents, and he had nestled down to rest, this little boy was accustomed, night after night, to rouse up once more, and to call out from his trundle-bed to his strong-armed father, in the room from which the light gleamed out, beyond the shadowy hallway, "Are you there, papa?" And the answer would come back cheerily, "Yes, my child, I am here." "You'll take care of me tonight, papa; won't you?" was then his question. "Yes, I'll take care of you, my child," was the comforting response. "Go to sleep now.

Good night." And the little fellow would fall asleep restfully, in the thought of those assuring good-night words.

A little matter that was to the loving father; but it was a great matter to the sensitive son. It helped to shape the son's life. It gave the father an added hold on him; and it opened up the way for his clearer understanding of his dependence on the loving watchfulness of the All-Father. And to this day when that son, himself a father and grandfather, lies down to sleep at night, he is accustomed, out of the memories of that lesson of long ago, to look up through the shadows of his earthly sleeping place into the far-off light of his Father's presence, and to call out, in the same spirit of childlike trust and helplessness as so long ago, "Father, you'll take care of me tonight; won't you?" And he hears the assuring answer back, "He that keepeth thee will not slumber. The LORD shall keep thee from all evil. He shall keep thy soul. Sleep, my child, in peace." And so he realizes the two-fold blessing of a father's good-night words.

A wise parent will prize and will rightly use the hour of the children's bedtime. That is the golden hour for good impressions on the children's hearts. That is the parent's choicest opportunity of holy influence. There should be no severity then, no punishment at that time. Every word spoken in that hour should be a word of gentleness and affection. The words which are most likely to be borne in mind by the children, in all their later years, as best illustrating the spirit and influence of their parents, are the good-night words of those parents. And it may be that those words are the last that the parents shall ever have the privilege of speaking to their children; for every night of sleep is a pregnant suggestion of the night of the last sleep. Let, then, the good-night words of parents to their children be always those words by which the parents would be glad to be remembered when their voices are forever hushed; and which they themselves can recall gladly if their children's ears are never again open to good-night words from them.

INDEX

Abraham as a child-trainer, 3.
Accidents, sympathy with children in, 153-54.
Adams, John Quincy, on the mother-love, 163-64.
Addison, Joseph, on reading, 103.
Affectation, of grief, for selfish ends, 56.
Afraid, when a child is old enough to be, 75-76.
Allowing play to a child's imagination, 167-70 (see Imagination).
Ambidextrous, gain of being, 32.
Amusements: training a child in, 91-96; necessary to children, 91; bad companionship to be avoided in, 93; should have no element of chance, 94; should not involve late hours, 94; a choice of reading in, 103-4.
Anger: never right in conference with a child, 22-23; never punish a child in, 121-27; defined, 121-22; confession by a parent of its influence on him, 123; its exhibit as "indignation" in punishing, 124-25; illustration of its evil on the mission-school superintendent, 125.
Animals: training better than breaking for them, 25-26; their knowledge through training, 83; gain of calmness in training them, 130.

Answering: a child's request deliberately, 60-61; a child's questions, importance of, 70-71; wise methods of, 71-73.
Apologizing, duty and manliness of, 101.
Appetite: early control of, possible, 56; training a child's, 63-68.
Assertion, self-, inconsistent with courtesy, 98.
Atmosphere, influence of the home, 155-58.

Bad Boy, the: some traits of, 122; example of, in a mission-school, 125.
Bashful child, the, 6.
Bedtime: a child's impressibility at, 177-78; a parent's irritability at, 178-80; mistakes of parents at, 179-80; illustrative memories of, 180-81.
Beginning: of training for a child, 3; of a child's self-control, 54.
Bending a child's will, distinguished from its breaking, 20.
Best things kept for Sunday, 85.
Bible study on Sunday is not always worship, 83.
Books [see Reading].
Braddock and Washington as contrasting cowardice and fear, 134.
Bravery consistent with fear, 134.

Breaking a child's will is never right, 20-27.

Bushnell, Horace: on giving a premium to a child's fretting, 55-56; on rewarding silence with "dainties," 55; on a parent's sympathy with a child's plays, 92-93; on the place for a parental explosion against evil, 124-25.

Candy: used wrongly, 55, 66-67; reserved for Sunday, 86.

Censure: few words better than many in, 130-31; a child's sorrow from a playmate's, 145; evil of unsympathetic, 152-53.

Centripetal force of some amusements, 94-95.

Chance, the element of, not admissible in children's amusements, 94.

Character: shaped by child training, 3-4; possibilities of, perceived, 40-41; shown in fears, 133-34.

Choice: faculty of, identified with the will, 20; God's dealings with men, on the basis of their freedom of, 20-21; not abrogated by rewards and punishments, 20-21; of obedience or punishment, a fair one, 22-24; for a child by parents, of studies and duties, 31-32; of food and drink, 63-64; of amusements, 91-92, 94-95; of reading, 103-4; of companionships, 115-16, 117-18; of a residence, school, a weekday school, or a Sunday school, 117.

Christ [see Jesus Christ].

Christian faith, the remedy for child-sorrows, 146-47.

Christmas: celebration of, may illustrate Sabbath observance, 84-85; distinguishing then between fact and fancy, 168-69; giving added value to a child's, 171-75.

Church services should be made attractive to children, 88-89.

Classic examples of table talk, 109-10.

Coaxing a child to be quiet, 550.

College curriculum, its value as a means of training, 31.

Comforting children by sympathy, 150.

Companionships: a child's amusements to be guarded, 93; guiding a child in, 115-19.

Condiments, a child's use of, 66-67.

Confession: of faults won through parental sympathy, 152-53; a child's readiness for, at bedtime, 177-78.

Conscientiousness, of young parents, as a cause of overdoing child training, 47-48.

Control [see Self-Control].

Conversation: honoring a child's interest in adult, 43-44; evil to a child of having himself for the topic of, 99-100, 101-2; favorable occasion for, at family meals, 110.

Counseling, not identical with training, 5.

Courtesy: training a child to, 97-102.

Cowardice, distinguished from fear, 133-34.

Criticism, of our children, by others, to be heeded, 15-16.

Crying: controlling by self-control, 54-55; not recognized as a means of gain, 59-60; a child's earliest action, 143.

Cultivating a child's taste for reading, 103-8 [see Reading].

Curbing, an element in training, 13-14.

Dark side of life, seen first by the child, 143.

David's recognition of the mother-love, 160.

Dealing tenderly with a child's fears, 133-41 [see Fears].

Death in the atmosphere, 155.

Definition: of training, 1; of teaching, 1-2; of faith, 75; of courtesy, 97; of good breeding, 98; of anger, 121; of punishment, 122; of scolding, 129; of sympathy, 149-50; of home atmosphere, 156; of the false and of the unreal, 167.

Denying: a child wisely, 33-37; not to be done hastily, 60-61.

De Quincey on "fine manners," 98.

Developmentally disabled children, their special lack, 7.

Diagnosis, important in parental care, as in medical practice, 14.

Dictionary, at hand for use in table talk, 112.

Discerning a child's special need of training, 13-17.

Discipline: by the use of "must" in child training, 29-30; example of Spartan, 37; danger of its overdoing, 47-48, 51-52; in eating and drinking, 63-64; in the mission-school, 125.

Dogs: to be trained, not broken, 26-27; a natural tone of voice in the training of, 130.

Dolls, as a child's treasure, 145-46.

Duty of training children, 5-7.

Education: begins with training rather than teaching, 1-2; progress in methods of, 30.

Eli honoring the child Samuel's individuality, 39-40.

English custom of separating parents and children at mealtime, 110-11.

Etiquette, distinguished from courtesy, 99-100.

Eton, influence of its playground on the battle of Waterloo, 94.

Ex post facto laws not justifiable, 126.

Eye and ear, trained by playthings and games, 93-94.

Fact and fancy, a child distinguishes between, 167.

Fairy tales: value and place of, 104-5; safer reading than falsely colored religious story-books, 169.

Faith, training a child's, 75-79.

Fancy and fact [see Fact].

Fathers sharing the amusements of children, 93.

Faults: of children, friends and neighbors may see those which

parents do not, 15-16; should excite parental sympathy, 152-53; children more ready to confess, at bedtime, 177-78.

Fears, dealing tenderly with a child's, 133-41.

Fiction: place and value of, in child's reading, 105; no place for the highly colored and overwrought, 106-7; when false is pernicious, 169-70.

First child, danger of overdoing the training of the, 48, 490.

Food: for children, should be chosen by parents, 63; inherited tastes for, may be overcome by training, 63-64; freaks of appetite for, 64-65; an American educator's method of training his children's tastes for, 66.

Forcing a child's will: never right, 20-22; permanent harm of, 25.

Freedom: of man's will, the basis of divine dealing, 20-21; to ask questions, limited, 71; should be permitted in family table talk, 112; from anxiety and sorrow not characteristic of childhood, 143.

Freshness of a child's thought on profound themes, 44, 76.

"Friend-enemies," parents as, according to Herbert Spencer, 153.

Games: for Sunday, 85-86; should be made a means of good, 93-94; the element of chance should be excluded from, 94; of an intellectual nature, 95; the right use of imagination in, 168.

Gentlemanliness, appealing to a boy's, 43.

Gentleness: in child training, 23; in dog-training, 25-26, 130; in managing a city mission-school, 125; in censuring, 130-31; in dealing with a child's fears, 133.

"Ghosts and goblins," in child-fears, 134-35, 140.

Gifts: abundance of, how unappreciated, 36; at Christmas,

valued in proportion to the giver's self going with them, 171, 174-75.

Gleason, the horse-trainer, methods of, 25-26.

Good breeding, defined, 98.

Good-night words, 177-81.

Gospel of John, as a first Bible book for South Sea Islanders, 76-77.

Grief: affectation of, for rewards, 55; freedom from, not characteristic of childhood, 143-44.

Guests, permitting children to sit at table with, 110.

Guiding a child in companionships, 115-19 [see Companionships].

Gullet, rubbing of the, a primitive custom, 3.

Habits: formed in infancy, 2-3, 53-54; affected by training, 11; should be regulated by parents, 30-31, 63-64, 64-65, 67-68.

Hagar, an example of the mother-love, 160.

Hammond, S. T., on dog-training, 25-26, 130.

Hannah, an example of the mother-love, 160.

Hasty denial of a child's request, unwise, 60-61.

History, a child trained to enjoy books of, 105-6.

Home: amusements of, should be a centripetal force, 94-95; to be made attractive, 95.

Home atmosphere, influence of, 94-95, 155-58.

Honoring a child's individuality, 9, 13, 19, 31, 39-45.

Horses trained, not broken, 25-26.

Illustrations: on the effects of training, 9-10; Johnny and his father, as to shutting the door, 22; a boy addressing a visitor by a familiar title, 23-24; from animal-training, 25-26, 130; flogging children on Innocents' Day, 29-30; the raisin-box wagon, 36; self-

denial of Spartans, 37; difference between clay and the living germ, 39-40; boy who knew better than his mother how sick he was, 42; boy who could not spare his watch, 42; stanzas from Wordsworth, 44; a young father over-disciplining his first child, 48, 49; "yanking" at the reins, 51; "I want to be pacified," 55; an American educator training the children's appetite for food, 66; Shetland ponies trained to eat hay, 67; Bishop Patteson among the South Sea Islanders, 76-77; a boy's rejoicing that Monday had come, 88; battle of Waterloo won on Eton's playground, 94; Fourth of July suggesting study of American history, 107; the table talk of famous guests, as a means of education, 111; lateral and perpendicular forces, 115-16; a parent who could punish only when angry, 123; a mission-school boy reproving his superintendent, 125; a child punished in love, responding with love, 126; Braddock and Washington in the presence of peril, 134; a baby who "doesn't like God's voice," 137; a father overcoming his child's fear of lightning, 137-38; power of imaginary fear over a strong man, 138-39; trusting God when afraid, 140; "Do robbers take dolls?" 145-46; a boy suicide, 146; from Herbert Spencer, on sympathy, 150-51; life and death in the atmosphere, 155; historical, of a mother's love, 159-66; of the play of a child's imagination, 167-68; of Christmas festivities, 172-75; "the old woman that lived in a shoe," 179; the boy calling from his "trundle-bed" to his father, 180.

Imagination: encouraging free play of a child's, 104; a cause of child-fears, 134; its part in the fears of the mature man, 136; distinguished from superstition, 139; to be appealed to, in overcoming such fears, 139-40; a child's, to be guarded from ghost stories, 140; allowing play to a child's, 167-70.

Imperfect development of every child, 7.

Improvements in school appliances, etc., 30.

Incarnation, disclosure of, in training child-faith, 78-79.

Inclination must submit to discipline, 31.

Indignation, in punishing, distinguished from anger, 124-25.

Influence of the home atmosphere, 155-58.

Innate, faith toward God is, but knowledge of him is not, 76.

"Innocents' Day," a time for flogging children, 29-30.

Instinctive: faith of every child, 76; fears, the value of, 136-37.

Interrogation point, a child as an animated, 69.

Issue with a child to be avoided as far as possible, 23-24, 49.

James and John, their mother's example of the mother-love, 161.

Jeroboam's wife, an example of the mother-love, 161.

Jesus Christ: incarnation of, readily grasped by a child's faith, 78-79; table talk of, 109-10; recognizing, on the cross, His mother's love, 160; sympathizes with our enjoyments, 175.

Jochebed, an example of the mother-love, 160.

John's Gospel as a first book for heathen converts, 76-77.

Johnson, Dr., on reading, 103; on the mother-love, 162.

Joyful observance of the Lord's Day, 82, 88-89.

Judgment, in judge or parent, should not be hasty, 121-22.

Kindergarten, a fundamental truth in its system, 93-94.

Knowledge: begins with a question, 69; questions should be directed in order to gain, 72; regarding God, must be disclosed to the child, 76.

Late hours, amusements of the child should not involve, 94.

Laughing: a time for, 56; not so easy, for a baby, as crying, 143.

Letting alone as a means of child training, 47-52.

Life: children see dark side of first, 143; burdens of, rest heaviest on the child-nature, 143-44; death and, in the atmosphere, 155.

Lightning and thunder, overcoming a child's fears of, 137-38.

Limitations: scope and, of child training, 9-12; to a child's privilege of question-asking, 71.

Lord's Day: every day is, 81; set apart from other days, in childish occupations, toys, etc., 84.

Love: God's, includes the bad child, 77; necessary to acceptable worship or work, 82; parental, in punishing, awakens child's, 126; distinguished from sympathy, 149-50, 153-54; an element of the home atmosphere, 157; the power of a mother's, 159-66; the divine compared with a mother's, 159-60; historical illustrations of, and testimonies to a mother's 159-66.

"Luck," no place for it in children's games, 94.

Luther, Martin: individuality of, in childhood, honored by Trebonius, 40-41; on the mother-love, 163.

Macaulay, Lord, on the mother-love, 164.

Making believe as distinct from deception, 167-68.

Manliness promoted by amusements, 94.

Manners, fine, according to De
     Quincey, 98.
Meals, mental and moral enjoyments
     at, 109-10.
Memory: of a mother's love, its
     permanent influence, 159;
     illustrated, 160-64; of Christmas
     festivities, 174; of the good-night
     kiss, 178.
Mental defects remedied, 10-11.
Misrepresenting God to a child, 77.
Mission-school, illustration of the
     bad boy in one, 125.
Moses, the possibilities of his
     character in infancy, 40.
Mother Goose, value of, 104-5.
Mother: has more time than the
     father to share children's
     amusements, 93; scolding by a, no
     better than an apple-woman's,
     129-30; commandments to honor,
     161.
Mother's love: the power of a,
     159-66; memory of, in the good-
     night kiss, 178.
Music in the home, 95.
"Must" the place of, in training,
     29-32 [see Discipline].

"Nagging" is not training, 51.
Napoleon Bonaparte, on the mother-
     love, 164.
Natural: objects, suggesting lines of
     reading, 107-8; tone of voice, in
     dog-training and in child training,
     130; power of sympathy not
     wholly, 153-54.
Neighbor's criticism of our children
     valuable, 15.
Never punish a child in anger, 121-27.
News, daily, outlined by father at
     breakfast table, 112.
Night [see Good-night Words].
Nonsense songs, value of, 104-5.
Nott, President, soothed at ninety by
     old lullabies, 163-64.

Observance of Sabbath, training a
     child to, 81-89.

"Only child, the": not always
     "spoiled," 34; disadvantage of his
     lack of companions at home, 116-17.
Opinions of a child, honoring the,
     44.
Overdoing in child training: danger
     of, 47; an error of the thoughtful
     as well as the thoughtless, 50-51.
Oxygen, analogy from, 155-56.

Parents: undervalue their power to
     train, 5, 16; blindness of, to the
     peculiar faults of their children, 14;
     should need criticism of neighbors
     and friends, 15-16; faults of, often
     reappear in their children, 16;
     should never force a child's choice,
     21; anger no help to, in training,
     22-23, 121; permanent harm to, in
     breaking their child's will, 25;
     should control a child's personal
     habits, 30-31; must often deny a
     child's requests, 33-34; must honor
     a child's individuality, 39; often
     inferior in possibilities to their
     children, 41; young, in danger of
     over-disciplining a child, 47;
     should seek to avoid direct issues
     with a child, 50; teaching the
     infant self-control, 54; training
     children to tease, 58; respect of,
     lost by children who tease, 59;
     giving sugar and condiments,
     66-67; average, unable to answer
     questions of average children,
     70-71; as revealers of revelation, 76;
     must have faith in order to train a
     child's faith, 79; should provide
     peculiar occupations and privileges
     for Sunday, 84, 86; should be the
     center of their children's
     amusements, 92,95; should learn
     from the kindergarten system, 94;
     should train children to courtesy,
     101; responsible for children's
     reading, 103, 105-6; should give
     children a share in family table
     talk, 110-11, 113-14; responsible for
     choice of a child's companions, 115,

117; should never punish in anger, 121; as peacekeepers and policemen, 124; should never scold, 129-30; should deal tenderly with child-fears, 133; should have sympathy for child-sorrows, 144-45; should point to Christ, as the way of comfort, 146-47; as "friend-enemies," 153; responsible for a home-atmosphere, 156-57; allowing play to a child's imagination, 167; should prepare for Christmas festivities, 171-72; the good-night words of, 177.

Passions and appetites, self-control of, should begin early, 54, 56.

Patience, necessity of: in dog-training and child training, 130; especially at child's bedtime, 178-79.

Patteson, Bishop, among the South Sea Islanders, 76-77.

Paul's self-control, 56.

Person, faith rests on a, 75.

Personal: power measured by willpower, 19; character to be held sacred, 20, 39; rights of children, honoring, 42; merit, not a means of acceptance with God, 77.

Physical: defects remedied, 10 11; pain, endurance of, 54-55.

Place of "must" in training, the, 29-32.

Place of sympathy in child training, 149-54.

Playmates: treatment of visiting, 100; unkindnesses of, 144 [see Companionships].

Playthings: use of, in training the faculties, 93-94; not a substitute for parental sympathy, 151; imagination in the use of, 168-69.

Politeness, true, 98.

Porter, President, on a college curriculum, 31.

Power of a mother's love, the, 159-66 [see Mother's Love].

Prayer: meaning of, taught before the child can talk, 76; faith in, not to supplant faith in God, 77; sharing a child's, 177-78; a new meaning of, gained through a child's good-night words, 181.

Preferences, personal: not to control study and work, 32; nor reading, 104.

Profound thought possible to a child, 44; as of God's personality and love, 76; or, the doctrine of the incarnation, 78-79.

Protection of a child, in danger, distinguished from punishment, 124.

Punish a child in anger, never, 121-27.

Punishment: divine, not destructive of free will, 21; teaching a child to choose obedience or, 22-23; undue severity of, 23; has a proper use, 121; should be a calm and judicial act, 121-22; distinguished from prompt protection of a child in danger, 124; administered in love, is recognized as love prompted, 126; often harder for a parent than for his child, 126; not to be inflicted upon an offense of ignorance, 126; child's permanent good the purpose of, 127; evil of postponing until the child's bedtime, 179.

Puzzles, for Sunday, 87.

Questioner, training a child as a, 69-73.

Questions: children encouraged to ask, 70; discouraged form asking improper, 71; value of a set time for answering, 72; should be in order to gain knowledge, 72; wisdom of deferring answers to some, 73; asking, in family table talk, 111-12.

Quiet talking more effective than scolding, 130-31.

Rachel, an example of the mother-love, 160.

Rarey, the horse-trainer, method of, 25-26.

Reading: cultivating a child's taste for, 103-8; its value, according to Addison and Johnson, 103; place and value of fiction in, 105; taste for good should be aroused in childhood, 105-6.

Reasonable fears to be met by reason, 136.

Recreation distinguished from amusement, 91.

Reference books, use of, in family table talk, 112.

Residence, companionships for children to be in mind, when choosing a, 117.

Respect, self-, of the courteous man, 98.

Rest, not in inaction, but in change, 82.

Rewards: divine use of, 20-21; dangers in the use of, 55.

Rich children in danger of being untrained in self-denial, 35.

Ridicule cannot overcome child-fears, 133-36.

Rizpah, an example of the mother-love, 160-61.

Romans, their tabletalk, 109.

Rubbing the gullet, a primitive custom, 3.

Sabbath, observance, training children to, 81-89.

Samuel's individuality, in childhood, honored by Eli, 40-41.

Santa Claus, as a Christmas fancy, 168-69.

Science, training a child to enjoy books of, 105-6.

Scolding: never in order, 129-31; most common at bedtime, 179.

Scope and limitations of child training, 9-12 [see Limitations].

Self-assertion not consistent with courtesy, 98.

Self-control: training a child to, 53-56; necessary for parents before punishing a child, 123-24; before censuring a child, 130-31.

Self-denial: importance of training children to, 33-34; an only child liable to lack stimulus to, 116-17.

Self-forgetfulness the basis of courtesy, 99.

Selfishness fostered by the granting of every request, 33-34.

Self-respect of the courteous man, 98.

Sermons for children, read at home on Sunday, 87.

Sharing: children's joys and sorrows, 150,152; children's Christmas pleasures, 175; in children's evening prayer, 177-78.

Shetland ponies trained to eat hay, 67.

Shunammite woman, an example of the mother-love, 161.

Silly questions not to be encouraged, 72.

Skelton, John, on scolding, 129.

Skill, not chance, in children's games, 94.

Soldier: fear felt by every, 134; imaginary fears of a, 136; finding peace on his deathbed through the mother-love, 165.

Solomon: on child training, 3; on honoring a mother, 161.

Sorrows of children, the: 143-47; they call for sympathy, 149-54; because of harsh treatment at bedtime, 178-79.

South Sea Islanders taught from John's Gospel first, 76-77.

Spartan children trained to self-denial, 37.

Special need of training, discerning a child's, 13-17.

Spencer, Herbert, on intellectual sympathy with children, 250-51.

Spoiled child, the: not always an "only child," 34; may be a first child, over-disciplined, 49.

Studying a child's specific needs, 16.

Sugar-plums to "pacify" crying children, 55, 64.

Suicide of children, 146.

Sunday school: lesson, studied at home on Sunday, 87; attendance of, in early childhood, 88; library book, mission of the average, 105; companionships in view while choosing a, 117.

Symmetry in child training, dependent on companionships, 116-17.

Sympathy: of parents with children in amusements, 92; in companionships, 116; in fears, 140; place of, in child training, 149-58; defined, 149-50, 153-54; Herbert Spencer on, 150-51; in a child's misdeeds and accidents, 152-53; not wholly natural to parents, 153-54; in the "home-atmosphere," 157; craved by a child at bedtime, 177-78.

Syro-Phoenician woman, an example of the mother-love, 161.

Table talk, the value of, 109-14.

Taste in reading, cultivating a child's, 103-8 [see Reading].

Teaching distinguished from training, 1.

Tease, training a child not to, 57-61.

Tenderly dealing with a child's fears, 133-41 [see Fears].

Thought, profound, possible to a child, 44.

Thoughtfulness for others, distinguished from self-forgetfulness, 99.

Thunder and lightening, overcoming a child's fears of, 137-38.

Timidity to be overcome by training, 135-36.

Timothy's mother, an example of the mother-love, 161.

Topics, assigning special, for next day's family table talk, 113.

Toys: for Sunday, 85-86; breaking of, a serious matter to a child, 145.

Training: distinguished from teaching, 1; defined, 1-2; should begin at birth, 3; shapes character, 3; more than counseling, 5; limited by a child's capacity, 9; special, necessary for every child, 13; danger of its developing the poorer self, 13; the child's will, 19; need of gentleness in, 22-23; by discipline, 29; a child to do unpleasant duties, 30, 32; by denying requests, 33-34; of an only child, 34; letting alone as a means of, 47-52; of a first child, 48-49; overdoing in, an error, 51; "nagging" is not, 51; to self-control, 53-56; not to tease, 57-61; Susannah Wesley's method of, 59-60; a child's appetite, 63-68; children as questioners, 69-73; a child's faith, 75-79; to Sabbath observance, 81-89; in amusements, 91-96; to courtesy, 97-102; a child's taste in reading, 103-8; value of table talk in, 110; child-companionships as an element in, 115-16; has no place for scolding, 129-31; tone of voice in, 130-31; by tenderness toward a child's fears, 133-41; joyousness as a result of, 143; sympathy as an aid in, 149-54; home atmosphere as a power in, 155-58; power of a mother's love in, 159-66; through the play of a child's imagination, 167-70; by good-night words and deeds, 177-81.

Trebonius, honoring the individuality of children, 40-41.

Trust: child's, is instinctive, 75-76; prayer is not mere asking, but 77-78.

"Tunge of a skolde," John Skelton's couplet on, 129.

Unselfishness: the basis of courtesy, 99; in a child's companionships, 116.

Value: of table talk, 109-14; giving added, to a child's Christmas, 171-75.

Values: child-sorrows measured by those of the child, 145.

Voice, necessity of natural tone of, in training, 130-31.

Wagon, raisin-box, 36.
Wanting not always reason for granting, 37.
Washington and Braddock as to fear, 134.
Watch, boy who could not spare his, 42.
Waterloo, battle of, won on Eton's playground, 94.
Wear, parents should decide what children may, 67.
Wellington, Duke of, quoted, 94.
Wesley, Susannah, her method in training, 59-60.
Whipping at bedtime, unwisdom of, 179.

Will, training of, rather than breaking, 19-27.
Wisdom: in denying a child, 33-37; more needed for letting alone than for commanding, 51.
Words, good-night [see Good-night].
Wordsworth, quoted, 44.
Worship: more than mere quietness in church, 82-83; family, on Sunday, 87.

"Yanking" at the reins is not good driving, 51.
Young: parents, in danger of over-disciplining, 47-48; teachers, peculiar influence of, 115; people, welcoming the mother's good-night kiss, 178.

ABOUT THE AUTHOR

Henry Clay Trumbull was born in Stonington, Connecticut, June 8, 1830. He became a world famous editor, author, and pioneer of the Sunday School Movement. Poor health kept him from formal education past the age of fourteen. Then his life was radically changed during revival meetings led by Charles Finney. What followed his conversion was truly a testimony of what God could do in the life of a yielded and willing servant.

During his lifetime he would become a world traveler, serve as Chaplain ministering to wounded in the Union Army, spend time in a Confederate prison, champion the cause and advancement of Sunday schools, become an expert Biblical archaeologist, become owner of the *Sunday School Times* magazine, write many books, become a sought-after speaker, and earn three honorary academic degrees from Yale, Lafayette, and New York University.

In spite of this busy schedule, he was a dedicated family man and raised eight children. Henry Clay Trumbull was sixty-years-old in 1890 when the wrote *Hints on Child Training*. This edition celebrates the one-hundredth anniversary of its first publication. Henry Clay Trumbull died in 1903 at the age of 73.

COLOPHON

The typeface for the text of this book is *Goudy Old Style*. Its creator, Frederic W. Goudy, was commissioned by American Type Founders Company to design a new Roman type face. Completed in 1915 and named Goudy Old Style, it was an instant bestseller. However, its designer had sold the design outright to the foundry, so when it became evident that additional versions would be needed to complete the family, the work was done by the foundry's own designer, Morris Benton. From the original design came seven additional weights and variants, all of which sold in great quantity. However, Goudy himself received no additional compensation for them. He later recounted a visit to the foundry with a group of printers, during which the guide stopped at one of the busy casting machines and stated, "Here's where Goudy goes down to posterity, while American Type Founders Company goes down to prosperity."

Cover Design:
Steve Diggs & Friends
Nashville, Tennessee

Page Composition:
Thoburn Press
P.O. Box 2459
Reston, Virginia 22090

Printing and Binding:
Versa Press, Inc.
E. Peoria, Illinois

Biographical Information:
Dean and Karen Andreola